D0596154

DAVID REAGAN THE MASTER PLAN

**MAKING SENSE OF
THE CONTROVERSIES
SURROUNDING
BIBLE PROPHECY
TODAY**

HARVEST HOUSE PUBLISHERS
Eugene, Oregon 97402

Copyright © 1993 by Lamb & Lion Ministries
P.O. Box 919, McKinney, Texas 75069
Published by Harvest House Publishers
Eugene, Oregon 97402

Library of Congress Cataloging-in-Publication Data

Reagan, David R., 1938–
    The master plan : making sense of the controversies
surrounding Bible prophecy today / David Reagan.
        p.   cm.
    ISBN 1-56507-074-7
    1. Bible—Prophecies.   2. Eschatology.   I. Reagan,
David R., 1938–   Down to earth insights into Bible
prophecy.   II. Title.
BS647.2.R434   1993
220.1'5—dc20   92-44138
                                            CIP

Printed in the United States of America.

Dedicated to
Mom and Pop Reagan

in appreciation for
their pointing me to Jesus

Preface

I'm tired of reading sensationalist prophecy books.

Because Bible prophecy deals with the future, it attracts curiosity seekers, and that in turn motivates sensationalists to write titillating books that appeal to the flesh rather than minister to the spirit.

Journalistic Prophecy

The book titles in the prophecy section of a typical Christian bookstore often smack of the same flavor as the headlines in the tabloids:

"Babylon Rebuilt!"
"Ark of the Covenant Discovered!"
"Vultures Gathering in Israel!"
"Computer Beast in Belgium!"
"Is Gorbachev Gog?"
"Could King Carlos Be the Antichrist?"
"The Mark of the Beast Is Here!"

On and on it goes, *ad nauseam*.

Prophecy Rumors

I recently received a letter from a radio listener who said her pastor had preached a whole sermon on a rumor he had heard from some prophecy teacher. The rumor, believe it or not, was that the building blocks of the next Jewish Temple have all been cut and numbered, and the blocks have been stored in K-Marts across the United States, waiting for the call to ship them to Jerusalem!

Bizarre rumors like this circulate constantly among prophecy buffs. It's enough to make a person conclude that the whole field of Bible prophecy is nothing but a playground for fanatics. Unfortunately, many Christians have come to that conclusion and have written off prophecy as a fruitful field for study.

That is too bad, for prophecy properly taught can be green pastures for disciples.

Purposes of This Book

This book addresses some of the basic concepts and issues in Bible prophecy in a nonsensationalist way. My purpose is not to stimulate the imagination but to feed the spirit.

The book aims to use God's Prophetic Word to motivate Bible study, to generate greater hope about the future, to encourage a commitment to holiness, and to develop a deeper relationship with Jesus.

It is also written to create a sense of urgency about the soon return of Jesus—and, more than that, a sense of expectancy.

Prophetic Apathy

Because the proper study of Bible prophecy has been so ignored in the modern-day Church, the average Christian is apathetic about the return of Jesus. The Bible says we are to yearn for the return of the Lord (2 Timothy 4:7-8). The Church today is yawning.

The proper biblical yearning can be found today primarily among the Orthodox Jews worldwide who are earnestly expecting the coming of the Messiah any moment. They sense His soon coming because they know the prophecies of the Hebrew Scriptures—what we call the Old Testament.

The Church, by contrast, is generally ignorant of Old Testament prophecies and has ignored or spiritualized New Testament prophecy.

The resulting paradox is that whereas the Jews failed to recognize the first coming of the Messiah, it is the Jews who are now attuned to the signs of the times while the Gentile Church seems blind.

As we will see in this book, God is currently performing one of His greatest miracles in history. The

Jews fully recognize it. The Church seems oblivious to it.

A Prayer

I pray this book will challenge and transform your thinking about the future by driving you deeper into God's Prophetic Word than you have ever dared to venture.

I pray the book will give you an appreciation for the fact that God is in control of history, that He has a master plan, and that He will orchestrate its fulfillment.

I pray too that the book will thrill your soul with the marvelous blessings God has promised His people in the future.

A Promise

I promise you that this study of prophecy will bless you. You may not agree with all I have to say, but you will be blessed by the promises of God that I will show you in the Scriptures.

The further you proceed in the book, the more you will come to fully appreciate the apostle Paul's statement in Romans 8:18—"I consider that the sufferings of this present time are not worthy to be compared with the glory that is to be revealed to us."

Maranatha!

—Dr. David R. Reagan

Contents

Introduction:
The Gate to Prophecy

The Eastern Gate in the old walled city of Jerusalem has a very special place in my heart, for it was that gate which God used to open my eyes to His Prophetic Word.

The year was 1967. The occasion was the Six-Day War. As the fate of the new state of Israel hung in the balance, I searched the newspapers daily for information about the war. The turning point came on June 7 when the Israeli army broke through the Lion's Gate and returned control of the ancient city of Jerusalem to the Jewish people for the first time in 1,897 years.

A Mysterious Remark

The next day I read a fascinating news account about one of the Jewish commando groups that had been involved in the assault on the city. The article stated that some members of the group had suggested catching the Jordanian defenders of the city off guard by blowing open the sealed Eastern Gate. But the leader of the group, an Orthodox Jew, had vehemently protested the idea, stating that "the Eastern Gate can be opened only when the Messiah comes."

That statement caught my eye; I wondered what the fellow was talking about. I knew nothing about the Eastern Gate except that it was the only gate of the city that led directly onto the Temple Mount. I was not aware that it was sealed, nor did I know that its opening was in any way biblically linked to the return of the Messiah.

A Remarkable Prophecy

I decided to do some research on the matter, and that decision initiated my study of Bible prophecy. I had been attending church for 30 years, but like most Christians, I knew nothing about Bible prophecy. The topic was generally ignored by the preachers in my boyhood church.

My concordance quickly directed me to the passage that the Orthodox Jew had alluded to: Ezekiel 44. The context is a supernatural tour which the Lord is giving Ezekiel of the future Millennial Temple (40:1-3).

In chapter 43 the Lord gives Ezekiel a vision of God's glory entering the Millennial Temple from the east, through the Eastern Gate. The Lord says to Ezekiel: "Son of man, this is the place of My throne and the place of the soles of My feet, where I will dwell among the sons of Israel forever" (43:7).

The Lord then reveals to Ezekiel that the Eastern Gate will be closed and will not be reopened until the Messiah returns in glory (44:1-3).

A Momentous Decision

The stage was set for the fulfillment of this prophecy more than 400 years ago in 1517 when the Turks conquered Jerusalem under the leadership of Suleiman the Magnificent. He commanded that the city's ancient walls be rebuilt, and in the midst of this rebuilding project, for some unknown reason, he ordered that the Eastern Gate be sealed up with stones.

Legends abound as to why Suleiman closed the gate. The most believable one is that while the walls were being rebuilt, a rumor swept Jerusalem that the Messiah was coming. Suleiman called together some Jewish rabbis and asked them to tell him about the Messiah. They described the Messiah as a great military leader who would be sent by God from the east. He would enter the Eastern Gate and liberate the city from foreign control.

Suleiman then decided to put an end to Jewish hopes by ordering the Eastern Gate sealed. He also put a Muslim cemetery in front of the Gate, believing that no Jewish holy man would defile himself by walking through a Muslim cemetery.

A Prophetic Symbol

The gate has remained sealed since that time and the Muslim cemetery still blocks the entrance. The old walled city has eight gates, and the Eastern Gate alone is sealed—just as prophesied in Ezekiel 44. The world would call that an "amazing coincidence." I call it a "God-incidence."

The Eastern Gate is proof positive that the Bible is the Word of God. Its sealing is clear evidence that we are living in the end times. The Gate awaits the return of the Messiah. Then and only then will it be opened.

A Vision

I have a vision of what that glorious day will be like. It is related to the Lord's First Coming. I believe Jesus is going to replay His triumphal entry into Jerusalem when He returns.

When He came the first time, Jesus rode a donkey from the Mount of Olives down into the Kidron Valley and up to the Eastern Gate, where He entered the Temple Mount for His last days of teaching. As He made that ride, the Valley of Kidron was filled with thousands of admirers who had heard about the resurrection of

Lazarus. They waved palm branches and chanted, "Hosanna to the Son of David!" Within a few days that same fickle crowd was shouting, "Crucify Him!"

We are told in Revelation 19 that when Jesus returns He will come as a victorious military conqueror, riding through the air on a supernatural white horse. In Isaiah 61 we are told that He will come from the east, and in Zechariah 14 we are told that He will touch ground on the Mount of Olives from which He ascended into Heaven.

Revelation 19:14 says that all the Redeemed will come with the Lord. Think of it! Those of us who are saved will be there to witness the Lord's return. Zechariah 14 says He will speak a word that will supernaturally destroy the Antichrist and his forces.

Then, I believe we will witness a replay of the Lord's triumphant entry into Jerusalem. With angels hovering above and millions of the Redeemed filling the Kidron Valley, Jesus will ride up to the Eastern Gate on His white horse, and as He approaches the Gate, it will open supernaturally. He will then enter the City of David, and to the triumphant shouts of "Hosanna to the Son of David," He will be crowned the King of kings and the Lord of lords.

I believe that's what Psalm 24:7-10 is all about when it says:

> Lift up your heads, O gates,
> And be lifted up, O ancient doors,
> That the King of glory may come in!
> Who is the King of glory?
> The LORD strong and mighty,
> The LORD mighty in battle....
> The LORD of hosts,
> He is the King of glory.

An Invitation

I invite you to enter the fascinating and spiritually enriching world of Bible prophecy with me. Allow me to be your guide to an overview of God's master plan for the future.

And as we proceed, remember to be a good Berean by testing everything I have to say against the Scriptures (Acts 17:10-11).

Prophetic Significance

*"We have the prophetic word made
more sure, to which you do well to pay
attention as to a lamp shining
in a dark place."*
—2 Peter 1:19

1

The Importance of Prophecy

Is It Just Pie in the Sky?

Although prophecy constitutes almost one-third of the Bible, its importance is constantly downplayed by those who dismiss it as lacking practical significance or by those who object to it as a fad that takes people's eyes off Jesus.

Revelation 19:10 says that "the testimony of Jesus is the spirit of prophecy." Thus, if prophecy is properly taught, there is no reason for it to divert anyone's attention away from Jesus. In fact, it should *emphasize* the centrality of Jesus.

Is prophecy practical? Consider that all the New Testament writers insist that the study of prophecy will motivate holy living. What could be more practical than that?

Prophecy does not have to be faddish, otherworldly, or impractical if taught properly. Nor does it have to be a playground for fanatics. It can and should be green pastures for disciples.

Reasons for Study

1. *Validator of Scripture*—Fulfilled prophecy is one of the best evidences I know of that the Bible is the inspired Word of God. The Bible contains hundreds of fulfilled secular prophecies pertaining to cities, nations, empires, and individuals. Jeremiah predicted the Babylonian captivity would last 70 years (Jeremiah 25:11-12). Isaiah stated that the children of Israel would be sent home from Babylon by a man named Cyrus (Ezra 1:1; Isaiah 44:28). Daniel foresaw the precise order of four great Gentile empires (Daniel 2 and 7). The destruction of Babylon was foretold by a number of the Hebrew prophets (e.g., Isaiah 13). In the New Testament, Jesus predicted the destruction of Jerusalem 40 years before it occurred (Luke 21:6).

2. *Validator of Jesus*—The Bible contains more than 300 prophecies about the First Coming of Jesus, all of which were literally fulfilled (see Appendix 1). Every aspect of the life of Jesus was prophesied: the place of His birth, the nature of His birth, the quality of His ministry, the purpose of His life, and the agony of His death. Consider, for example, the prophecy in Psalm 22:16 that the Messiah's hands and feet would be pierced. That prophecy was written by David about a thousand years before the birth of Jesus. It was written 700 years before the invention of crucifixion as a form of execution. The literal fulfillment of so many prophecies in the life of one individual transcends any mere coincidence and serves to validate that Jesus was who He said He was—the divine Son of God.

3. *Revealer of the Future*—Prophecy tells us some things God wants us to know about the future (Deuteronomy 29:29; Amos 3:7). God does not want us to

know everything about the future, but there are some things we must know if we are to have a dynamic hope. Thus, prophecy assures us that Jesus is coming back, that He will resurrect us, and that He will take us to live forever with Him and God the Father. In this regard, Peter likens prophecy to "a lamp shining in a dark place" (2 Peter 1:19). Paul makes the same point in 1 Corinthians chapter 2. He begins by observing that no eye has seen, no ear has heard, nor has the mind of man conceived, what God has prepared for those who love Him. But in the next verse Paul says those things have been revealed to us by God through His Spirit (1 Corinthians 2:9-10).

4. *Tool of Evangelism*—Prophecy can be used as an effective tool of evangelism, as illustrated in the story of Philip and the eunuch (Acts 8:26ff.). Philip used Isaiah's great suffering lamb passage (Isaiah 53) to teach that Jesus is the Lamb who was slain for the sins of the world. Matthew and Peter both used fulfilled prophecy in the life of Jesus as one of their basic evangelistic tools. In fact, Peter referred to prophecy constantly in his first gospel sermon on the Day of Pentecost (Acts 2:14-39). He preached that Jesus had been crucified and resurrected in fulfillment of Hebrew prophecies. Later, Peter referred to fulfilled prophecy as one of the greatest evidences that Jesus was truly the Son of God (2 Peter 1:16-19).

5. *Tool of Moral Teaching*—People often overlook the fact that the Hebrew prophets were *forth*tellers as well as *fore*tellers. In fact, the prophets spent most of their time using God's Word to spotlight societal problems. They called their listeners to repentance, true worship, social justice, and personal holiness. One of the great recurring themes of the prophets is that obedience is better than sacrifice (1 Samuel 15:22 and Hosea 6:6). That statement means that in God's eyes, obedience to

His commands is more important than outward religious practices such as offering sacrifices. Prophecy is thus a great repository of moral teaching, and those moral principles are still relevant today. (See Amos 5:21-24; Micah 6:8; Isaiah 58:3-9.)

6. *Generator of Spiritual Growth*—Prophetic knowledge encourages patient waiting (James 5:7-8); provokes earnest watching (Matthew 24:36,42); inspires dedicated work (2 Timothy 4:7-8); and enhances our hope (Titus 2:11-14). The result is holy living. Paul exhorts us to "behave properly as in the day," because the time is at hand when the Lord will return (Romans 13:12-13). Likewise, Peter calls us to gird up our minds and be sober and holy as we look forward to the revelation of Jesus (1 Peter 1:13-15).

Advice and Counsel

In 2 Timothy 3:16-17 Paul writes that *all* of God's Word is "profitable for teaching, for reproof, for correction, for training in righteousness." That includes God's Prophetic Word. In 1 Thessalonians 5:20 the apostle Paul pleads with us to treat prophecy with respect.

Peter warns us in his second epistle that one of the signs of the end times will be the appearance of scoffers who will cast scorn and ridicule on the promise of our Lord's return (2 Peter 3:3ff.). The great tragedy of our day is that many of the loudest scoffers are religious leaders who profess to follow Christ. Such leaders crucified Jesus the first time He came. They now scoff at His promise to return.

A good example is the "Jesus Seminar" that has been operating for the past few years. It is composed of 40 New Testament "scholars" from a great variety of Christian seminaries in America. The seminar has been meeting every six months to vote on the sayings of Jesus as recorded in the four gospels. They hope to produce a new version of the gospels in which the sayings of Jesus will be color coded: red, if He said it; pink, if He may have said it; gray, if He probably did not say it; and black, if He definitely did not say it.

When they voted on the sayings of Jesus regarding His Second Coming, they voted that *all* the sayings were spurious and had probably been invented by His disciples. What apostasy!

Spiritual Food

God's Prophetic Word is food for our spiritual growth. We need to take it off the shelf. We need to open it up and feast upon it, and we need to do so with believing hearts.

The book of Revelation promises blessings to those who read it (or hear it read) and who obey it (Revelation 1:3). It is the only book of the Bible to promise such a specific blessing, even though all God's Word (including every prophetic passage) is designed to bless us spiritually (Psalm 119).

Key Scriptures about Prophecy

Before we get to the meat of our study, let's remind ourselves what the Word of God itself says about the value of prophecy. In this way we can be assured that the effort we expend in looking at the prophetic Scriptures will be time extremely well spent.

> The secret things belong to the LORD our God; but the things revealed belong to us and to our sons forever (Deuteronomy 29:29).

> Surely the LORD God does nothing unless He reveals His secret counsel to His servants the prophets (Amos 3:7).

> I am God, and there is no other; I am God, and there is no one like Me, declaring the end from the

beginning and from ancient times things which have not been done.... I have spoken; truly I will bring it to pass. I have planned it, surely I will do it (Isaiah 46:9-11).

[Jesus said] Do not think that I came to abolish the Law or the Prophets; I did not come to abolish, but to fulfill (Matthew 5:17).

[Jesus] said to them, "These are My words which I spoke to you while I was still with you, that all things which are written about Me in the Law of Moses and the Prophets and the Psalms must be fulfilled" (Luke 24:44).

Of Him [Jesus] all the prophets bear witness that through His name every one who believes in Him receives forgiveness of sins (Acts 10:43).

The prophets who prophesied of the grace that would come to you made careful search and inquiry, seeking to know what person or time the Spirit of Christ within them was indicating as He predicted the sufferings of Christ and the glories to follow (1 Peter 1:10-11).

Know this first of all, that no prophecy of Scripture is a matter of one's own interpretation, for no prophecy was ever made by an act of human will, but men moved by the Holy Spirit spoke from God (2 Peter 1:20-21).

The testimony of Jesus is the spirit of prophecy (Revelation 19:10).

2

The Abuse
of Prophecy

Does It Deserve Contempt?

Let's face it—prophecy is held in contempt by most people.

Non-Christians scoff at the very idea of supernatural knowledge about the future. The ironic thing is that in doing so they fulfill a prophecy of Peter: "In the last days mockers will come with their mocking, following after their own lusts, and saying, 'Where is the promise of His coming?'" (2 Peter 3:3-4).

The Apostates

The real tragedy concerning God's Prophetic Word is that so many Christians share this same scoffing attitude. Apostate Christian seminaries have pretty well rejected the whole concept of prophecy. Most now teach that prophecy is really history written after the fact but written like prophecy to make it more interesting.

27

This rejection of prophecy on the part of apostate Christians is a natural outgrowth of their worship at the manmade altar of what theologians call "historical criticism."

This despicable methodology rejects the Bible as God's revelation to Man, arguing instead that it represents Man's faltering search for God. Its proponents have concluded that the Bible is full of myth, superstition, and legend.

Since they have rejected the supernatural, these people cannot accept the idea of prophecy as revealed pre-knowledge of history. This is why the book of Daniel has been a focus of their scorn and ridicule. It is not at all unusual to hear one of their scholars say, "The book of Daniel is just too accurate. It had to be written after the events it claims to prophesy." This is nothing but blatant unbelief which calls into question our Lord's own acceptance of Daniel as authentic (Matthew 24:15).

This attitude is also a fulfillment of prophecy, for Jesus said that in the end times there will be a great apostasy within the professing Church (Matthew 24:10-12). As Paul put it, the end times will be marked by men "holding to a form of godliness, although they have denied its power" (2 Timothy 3:5).

The Spiritualizers

Prophecy has also suffered abuse at the hands of those who have specialized in spiritualizing it. Liberals and conservatives both have been guilty of this practice.

"Spiritualizing" refers to any methodology which holds that prophecy does not mean what it says. In practice this always leads to a symbolic interpretation of prophecy. The plain-sense meaning of prophecy is denied, and prophetic books like Revelation are treated like they were adult *Alice in Wonderland* books with a vague, general message but no specific meaning.

This spiritualization of prophecy on the part of *liberals* is easy to understand. It is a natural extension of their tendency to spiritualize all of Scripture. They have spiritualized the miracles of God in the Old Testament and the miracles of Jesus in the New Testament, so why should they accept the plain-sense meaning of prophecy, especially when it teaches a supernatural consummation of history?

It's the *conservative* spiritualizers who are such a mystery to me. They accept the Bible as the Word of God. They agree that the Bible contains supernatural revelations about the future. They interpret virtually all nonprophetic passages literally. They even interpret the First Coming prophecies literally. Yet they insist upon spiritualizing all the Bible's prophecies concerning the Second Coming.

Thus, they deny the coming reality of the Tribulation, the Millennial Reign, and the New Earth. They take a passage such as Zechariah 14, which says Jesus will return to the Mount of Olives and reign on the earth, and they spiritualize it to mean that when you accept Jesus as Lord and Savior, He comes into your heart (the Mount of Olives) and begins to reign in your life (the reign on earth). Such people should be granted Ph.D.'s in imagination!

If the prophecies concerning the First Coming of Jesus were all fulfilled in some literal way in their plain-sense meaning, then why shouldn't the Second Coming prophecies be fulfilled the same way?

The Apathetic

Then there are those Christians who are simply apathetic about prophecy. They couldn't care less.

Many of these Christians think prophecy has no practical relevance to their daily lives, so they ignore it. They have never read the Major Prophets. They couldn't even find the Minor Prophets. And they certainly aren't going to waste their time with that "Chinese puzzle" called the book of Revelation.

My own church heritage fits this description. Our apathetic attitude was motivated by the peculiar belief that all Old Testament prophecy had been fulfilled and therefore the study of prophecy was a waste of time.

Other Christians have become apathetic about prophecy because it has been so badly abused by fanatical sensationalists, especially date-setters. These Christians are weary of weird interpretations that have brought reproach to the Body of Christ.

Even as I write this paragraph, the newspapers are trumpeting stories about two groups, one in Korea and one in America, which have gained international headlines by predicting the Lord would come back in the past few days. The dates they set have passed. We're still here. And the world laughs.

Another cause of apathy is that many people have been turned off by the specialized vocabulary of prophecy. When they hear technical terms like "premillennial," "postmillennial," and "amillennial," their eyes roll back in their heads and they space out, concluding that prophecy is a field of study for experts only.

The Fanatics

Finally, there are the fanatics. These are the people who apply their fertile imaginations to prophecy and then speculate and theorize all sorts of fanciful future events.

They usually are obsessed with date setting or speculating about whether or not a person like Henry Kissinger is the Antichrist.

Often they are rumor mongers who spread wild stories about vultures gathering in Israel, Belgian computers taking over the world, the Jews collecting building blocks for the Temple, the Social Security Administration stamping numbers on people's hands, and Jane Fonda's name having the numerical equivalent of 666!

A Satanic Conspiracy

I believe that Satan himself has inspired all this abuse of God's Prophetic Word. Satan does not want anyone studying prophecy, because prophecy contains the revelation of Satan's ultimate and total defeat.

Satan used to defeat me all the time by constantly reminding me of my past sins. But my study of Bible prophecy has given me a new weapon to fight back with. Now, every time Satan reminds me of my past, I remind him of his future! He responds by sulking away in defeat.

The book of Revelation begins with the words, "The *Revelation* of Jesus Christ." The book of Revelation, like the rest of prophecy, is meant to reveal the future. It is meant to be understood. God wants to build our hope in the midst of a dark and troubled world by revealing to us the great victories that lie ahead in His master plan.

I exhort you to stand firm against Satan in his attempt to convince you that God's Prophetic Word is not to be taken seriously.

3

The Range of Prophecy

Is It Only in Written Form?

Hebrews 1:1 says that God spoke through the prophets "in many portions and in many ways." Have you ever stopped to think about the variety of people and ways which God used?

Writing Prophets

Of course, the method that immediately comes to mind is the written form. The prophets who wrote down their messages are the ones we know best—people like Isaiah, Jeremiah, Ezekiel, Daniel, and the so-called "Minor Prophets" like Habakkuk and Zephaniah. In the New Testament the writing prophets include Paul, Peter, and John.

But to lump all these writing prophets together into one broad category is misleading, for there is a great variety of people and styles among them.

As to people, the variety is astounding. The prophets range from uneducated farmers like Amos to sophisticated poets like Isaiah, from reluctant spokesmen like Jonah to men of great courage like Daniel, from the little known like Joel to the famous like King David.

There is an equal variety in the styles of writing. Some, like Ezekiel, Daniel, Haggai, and the New Testament prophets, primarily used a prose style. Others, like David, Isaiah, Joel, and Micah, expressed their ideas mostly in poetic form. And then there are the preachers whose books are mainly collections of sermons—prophets like Jeremiah, Amos, and Zechariah.

Most were given direct revelations: "Thus says the Lord." Others received their insight through dreams and visions. Some, like Hosea and Jonah, simply recorded their experiences.

Speaking Prophets

Some of the most important prophets wrote nothing at all, at least nothing that has been preserved. We know about them because others wrote about their revelations, pronouncements, and exploits. Elijah and his successor, Elisha, fall into this category, as does Samuel.

So does the greatest prophet who ever lived—*the* Prophet foretold by Moses (Deuteronomy 18:15-18). I'm speaking, of course, of Jesus Christ (Matthew 21:11). The only writings of Jesus that we have are His seven letters to the seven churches of Asia, recorded by John in Revelation 2 and 3. The bulk of Jesus' prophecies, such as His Olivet Discourse (Matthew 24; Mark 13; Luke 21), were written by His disciples. Jesus was an oral prophet.

Most of the oral prophets are not well known. Only a few are mentioned in the New Testament—such as the four daughters of Philip (Acts 21:9) and Agabus, the prophet who counseled Paul (Acts 21:10).

But the Old Testament is full of oral prophets. There is Nathan, who confronted David (2 Samuel 12); Micaiah, who saw the Lord sitting on His throne (1 Kings 22); Ahijah, who condemned Jeroboam (1 Kings 14); Hananiah, the false prophet who spoke against Jeremiah (Jeremiah 28); and many nameless prophets such as the "man of God from Judah" who prophesied the birth of Josiah (1 Kings 13).

Acting Prophets

My favorites are the prophets who were called upon by God to act out prophecies. Some were writing prophets; some were oral. From time to time God would tell them to stop writing or speaking and start acting.

God often used drama to get people's attention. For example, He told Isaiah to go barefoot and naked for three years (Isaiah 20:2ff.). Yes, Isaiah was the original streaker! He used an unconventional method to get people's attention. The message was graphic and clear: Repent or be stripped naked like Isaiah.

Jeremiah was told to wear a yoke on his neck to emphasize God's message that King Zedekiah should submit to Nebuchadnezzar (Jeremiah 27).

Ezekiel was called on to act many times. On one occasion the Lord told him to pack all his bags and carry them around Jerusalem in the sight of the people as a sign that if they did not repent, God would send them into exile (Ezekiel 12). On another occasion God ordered Ezekiel to play in a sand pile! God told him to label a brick "Jerusalem" and to build dirt ramps around the brick to illustrate the coming siege of the city, if the people did not repent (Ezekiel 4).

The Prophetic Oscar

The greatest actor of all, the one who will undoubtedly win the prophetic Oscar for best performance, was the prophet Hosea.

God told him to find a prostitute and marry her. It must have been one of the hardest things God ever asked a righteous man to do. Hosea obeyed, and God told him to preach the message of his action.

The message was that Israel was like that prostitute when God selected the nation as His Chosen People. They were not selected for their beauty or wisdom or righteousness. They had no merit of their own. They were selected by grace.

This was an insulting message for the Jews. They did not understand what being "chosen" meant. They thought they were better than other peoples, and in their spiritual arrogance they refused to listen to God's prophets who were calling for repentance.

When Hosea returned home from his preaching tour, he discovered that his wife had succumbed to her old passions. She had left the dignity and honor of his home and had returned to the streets, selling herself to the highest bidder. Hosea's heart was broken. God told him to preach the message of her action. The message was that, like Hosea's wife, Israel had been unfaithful to God, chasing after foreign gods. And like Hosea, God's heart was broken.

When Hosea returned home, God spoke to him again and asked him to do something incredible. God told him to swallow all his pride and go to the city square and bid for his wife when she offered herself for sale. He was instructed to pay all he had, if necessary, to redeem her from harlotry.

She didn't deserve it. She had not repented. But Hosea obeyed. He paid the price, and she was redeemed.

In this manner, God used an acting prophet to act out the story of what He would do for us at the Cross when He paid the price of His Son to redeem us from our unfaithfulness.

Symbolic Prophecy

A fourth type of prophecy is symbolic prophecy, or what is often referred to as "prophecy in type."

An understanding of prophetic types is essential to understanding the Old Testament. Jesus can be found on almost every page of the Old Testament, if you know how to look for Him. He is there symbolically in types. Looking for Him and finding Him in these types causes the Old Testament to come alive. I'm convinced that this is the kind of special teaching that Jesus gave His disciples during the 40 days between His resurrection and His ascension (Luke 24:45).

There are three kinds of prophetic types: 1) individual lives; 2) historical events; and 3) inanimate objects.

Persons as Types

Almost all the major persons in the Old Testament are types of Christ in the sense that some events in their lives prophesied things that would happen to Jesus.

Joseph, for example, was rejected by his brothers. He was left for dead but was "resurrected" from the pit into which he had been cast. He took a Gentile bride and then redeemed his brothers from their famine.

Likewise, Jesus was rejected by His brethren (the Jews), experienced death and resurrection, is now taking a Gentile bride (the Church), and will soon return to save a remnant of His brethren from their spiritual famine.

Symbolic Events

Prophecies about Jesus are also symbolized in major historical events.

Take the seven feasts of Israel as an example. Jesus was crucified on the Feast of Passover. He became our "unleavened bread" as His body rested in the ground on

that feast day. He arose from the dead on the Feast of
Firstfruits. And the Church was established on the
Feast of Pentecost.

The three unfulfilled feasts (Trumpets, Atonement,
and Tabernacles) likewise must point to events that are
yet to occur—most likely, the Rapture, the Second Coming, and the Millennial Reign of Jesus.

The history of the Jewish nation is the story of Jesus
in prophetic type. The Children of Israel were born in
Canaan, descended into Egypt, came through the Red
Sea (the baptism of Moses), endured testing in the wilderness, and then entered the Promised Land.

Likewise, Jesus was born in Canaan, descended into
Egypt, emerged publicly at His baptism, endured the
wilderness temptations, and led the way to Heaven.

The Significance of Objects

Even inanimate objects like the Tabernacle and the
robe of the High Priest are prophetic types pointing to
Jesus.

Consider the Ark of the Covenant. Everything
about it was symbolic of the Messiah. It was made of
wood, indicating the Messiah would be human. It was
overlaid with gold, signifying the Messiah would be
divine. It contained three objects—the tablets of stone,
a pot of manna, and Aaron's rod that budded. The tablets signified that the Messiah would have the Law of
God in His heart. The manna meant the Messiah would
be the Bread of Life. The rod with blooms was a prophecy
that the Messiah would arise from the dead.

The lid of the Ark was called the Mercy Seat. It had a
golden angel at each end. The angels faced each other
and their wings hovered over the lid. Once a year the
High Priest sprinkled blood on the Mercy Seat and
communed with the Shekinah glory of God which hovered above the angels.

The Mercy Seat pointed to the fact that through the work of the Messiah the mercy of God would cover the Law. The blood foreshadowed the fact that the Messiah would have to shed His own blood to atone for our sins.

Jesus fulfilled every prophetic type of the Ark. He was God in the flesh (John 10:30). He had the Law in His heart (Matthew 5:17). He declared Himself to be the "Bread of Life" (John 6). He shed His blood on the Cross and was resurrected in power, atoning for our sins and covering the Law with Grace (Romans 3:21-26).

Mary saw the fulfillment of the Ark when she went to the tomb and discovered the body of Jesus missing. John 20:11-12 says she looked into the tomb and "beheld two angels in white sitting, one at the head, and one at the feet, where the body of Jesus had been lying." Do you understand what she saw? She saw the "mercy seat" where the blood had been spilled, with an angel at each end—exactly like the Mercy Seat that covered the Ark!

An Exhortation

I hope this brief overview demonstrates how prophetic types bring the Old Testament alive and give us deep insight into New Testament events.

I encourage you to read the Bible with an attitude of always looking for Jesus. He is there on every page, waiting for you to discover Him in the symbols and types.

Pray for the guidance of the Holy Spirit as you read, and remember Revelation 19:10: "The testimony of Jesus is the spirit of prophecy."

4

The Interpretation of Prophecy

Imagination or Plain Sense?

When I was about 12 years old, I stumbled across Zechariah 14. It was an amazing discovery.

You see, I grew up in a church where we were told over and over that "there is not one verse in the Bible that even implies that Jesus will ever set His feet on this earth again."

Simple Language

Well, Zechariah 14 not only implies that the Lord is coming back to this earth again, it says so point-blank! It says that the Lord will return to this earth at a time when the Jews are back in the land of Israel and their capital city, Jerusalem, is under siege. Just as the city is about to fall, the Lord will return to the Mount of Olives.

When His feet touch the ground, the mount will split in half. The remnant of Jews left in the city will

41

take refuge in the cleavage of the mountain. The Lord will then speak a supernatural word, and the armies surrounding Jerusalem will be destroyed in an instant.

Verse 9 declares that on that day "the LORD will be king over all the earth."

Muddled Interpretations

When I first discovered this passage, I took it to my minister and asked him what it meant. I will never forget his response. He thought for a moment, and then he said, "Son, I don't know what it means, but I'll guarantee you one thing: It doesn't mean what it says!"

For years after that, I would show Zechariah 14 to every visiting evangelist who came preaching that Jesus would never return to this earth. I always received the same response: "It doesn't mean what it says." I couldn't buy that answer.

Finally, I ran across a minister who was a seminary graduate, and he gave me an answer I could live with. "Nothing in Zechariah means what it says," he explained, "because the whole book is apocalyptic."

Now, I didn't have the slightest idea what "apocalyptic" meant. I didn't know if it was a disease or a philosophy. But it sounded sophisticated, and, after all, the fellow was a seminary graduate, so he should know.

A Discovery Experience

When I began to preach, I parroted what I had heard from the pulpit all my life. When I spoke on prophecy, I would always make the point that Jesus will never return to this earth. Occasionally, people would come up after the sermon and ask, "What about Zechariah 14?" I would snap back at them with one word: "APOCALYPTIC!" They would usually run for the door in fright. They didn't know what I was talking about (and neither did I).

Then one day I sat down and read the whole book of Zechariah. And guess what? My entire argument went down the drain!

I discovered that the book contains many prophecies about the First Coming of Jesus, and I discovered that all those prophecies meant what they said. It suddenly occurred to me that if Zechariah's *First* Coming prophecies meant what they said, then why shouldn't his *Second* Coming promises mean what they say?

The Plain-Sense Rule

That was the day that I stopped playing games with God's Prophetic Word and started accepting it for its plain-sense meaning. I decided that if the plain sense makes sense, I would look for no other sense, lest I end up with nonsense.

A good example of the nonsense approach is one I found several years ago in a book on the Millennium. The author spiritualized all of Zechariah 14. He argued that the Mount of Olives is symbolic of the human heart surrounded by evil. When a person accepts Jesus as Savior, Jesus comes into the person's life and stands on his "Mount of Olives" (his heart). The person's heart breaks in contrition (the cleaving of the mountain), and Jesus then defeats the enemy forces in the person's life.

Hard to believe, isn't it? When someone insists on spiritualizing the Scriptures like this, the Scriptures end up meaning whatever the interpreter wants them to mean.

Keys to Understanding

I believe God knows how to communicate. I believe He says what He means and means what He says. I don't believe you have to have a doctorate in hermeneutics to understand the Bible. The essentials, instead, are an honest heart and the filling of God's Spirit (1 Corinthians 2:10-16).

One crucial key is to approach the Scriptures with childlike faith. Dr. Henry Morris addresses this issue in his great commentary on Revelation, *The Revelation Record*. He says, "Revelation is not difficult to understand. It is difficult to believe. If you will believe it, you will understand it."

For example, Revelation 7 teaches that at the start of the Tribulation God is going to seal a great host of Jews to serve as His special "bond-servants." The text specifies that the number will be 144,000, and that 12,000 will be selected from each of 12 specified tribes.

Now I ask you: What would God have to do to convince us that He intends to set aside 144,000 Jews for special service during the Tribulation? The text is crystal clear. Yet hundreds of commentators have denied the clear meaning and have spiritualized the passage to make it refer to the Church! This is reckless handling of God's Word and it produces nothing but confusion.

The Meaning of Symbols

"But what about symbols?" some ask. Another crucial key to keep in mind is that a symbol stands for something, otherwise it would not be a symbol. There is always a literal reality or plain-sense meaning behind every symbol.

Jesus is called "the rose of Sharon." He is not referred to as "the tumbleweed of Texas." The image that a rose conjures up is something beautiful; a tumbleweed is ugly.

The Bible is its own best interpreter of the symbols it uses. Sometimes the symbols are clearly explained, as when God reveals to Ezekiel the meaning of the symbols in his vision of the valley of dry bones (Ezekiel 37:11-14). In like manner, the apostle John was told the meaning of certain symbols which he saw in his Patmos vision of the glorified Lord (Revelation 1:20).

At other times a simple search of the Scriptures will reveal the meaning of a symbol. Consider the statement in Revelation 12:14 which says that the Jewish remnant will escape from the Antichrist into the wilderness on "the two wings of the great eagle."

Is this a literal eagle? Is it an airlift provided by the U.S.A., whose national symbol is an eagle?

A concordance search will show that the same symbolism is used in Exodus 19:4 to describe the flight of the children of Israel as they escaped from Egypt. The symbol, as Exodus 19 makes clear, is a poetic reference to the loving care of God.

The Importance of Context

Another key to understanding prophecy applies to the interpretation of *all* Scripture as well. It is the principle that the meaning of words is determined by their context.

I ran across a good example of this problem recently in a book in which the author was trying to prove that Jesus is never coming back to reign upon this earth. Such a position, of course, required him to spiritualize Revelation chapter 20, where it says six times that there will be a reign of the Lord that will last 1,000 years.

In this author's desperate attempt to explain away the thousand years, he referred to Psalm 50:10, which says that God owns "the cattle on a thousand hills." He then asked, "Are there only one thousand hills in the world?" He answered his question, "Of course not!" He then proceeded to explain that the term is used figuratively. But then he made a quantum leap in logic by proclaiming, "Therefore, the term, 'one thousand,' is always used symbolically."

Not so. It depends on context. In Psalm 50 the term is clearly symbolic. But in Revelation 20, it is not so. The thousand years is mentioned there *six times*. What would the Lord have to do to convince us that He means a thousand years? Put it in the sky in neon lights? Pay attention to context!

Reconciling Passages

The next key to understanding prophecy also applies to all of Scripture, as did the previous one. It is the principle of searching out everything that the Bible has to say on a particular point.

Avoid hanging a doctrine on one isolated verse. All verses on a particular topic must be searched out, compared, and then reconciled.

Let me give you a prophetic example. Second Peter 3:10 says that when the Lord returns, "the heavens will pass away with a roar...and the earth and its works will be burned up." Now, if this were the only verse in the Bible about the Second Coming, we could confidently conclude that the heavens and earth will be burned up on the day that Jesus returns.

But there are *many* other verses in both the Old and New Testaments which make it abundantly clear that the Lord will reign over all the earth before it is consumed with fire. Those verses must be considered together with the passage in 2 Peter 3 in order to get the correct overall view.

Special Problems

There are some special problems related to prophetic interpretation. One is that prophecy is often pre-filled in symbolic type before it is completely fulfilled.

I feel certain that the Jewish people must have felt that Antiochus Epiphanes fulfilled Daniel's prophecies about a tyrannical leader who would severely persecute the Jews. But 200 years after Antiochus, Jesus took those prophecies of Daniel and told His disciples they were yet to be fulfilled.

Another example is the sign which Isaiah gave to King Ahaz to assure him that the city of Jerusalem would not fall to the Syrians who had it under siege. The sign was that a young woman would give birth to a son whose name would be called Immanuel (Isaiah 7:1-19). The passage certainly implies that such a boy was born at that time.

But hundreds of years later, Matthew, by inspiration of the Holy Spirit, reached back to Isaiah's prophecy and proclaimed that its ultimate fulfillment was to be found in the virgin birth of Jesus (Matthew 1:22-23).

Compressed Time

Another peculiar feature of prophetic literature is called "telescoping." This occurs when a prophet compresses the time interval between two prophetic events. This phenomenon is very common.

The reason for it has to do with the perspective of the prophet. As he looks into the future and sees a series of prophetic events, they appear to him as if they are in immediate sequence.

It is like looking down a mountain range and viewing three peaks, one behind the other, each sequentially higher than the one in front of it. The peaks look like they are right up against each other because the person viewing them cannot see the valleys that separate them.

In Zechariah 9:9-10 there is a passage with three prophecies which are compressed into two verses but which actually are widely separated in time. Verse 9 says the Messiah will come humbly on a donkey. The first part of verse 10 says the Jewish people will be set aside. The second part of verse 10 says the Messiah will reign over all the nations.

These three events—the First Coming, the setting aside of Israel, and the reign of Christ—appear to occur in quick succession, but in reality there were 40 years between the first two events and there have been over 1,900 years thus far between the second and third events.

Another way of viewing the phenomenon of telescoping is to focus on what are called "prophetic gaps." These are the time periods between the mountain peak prophetic events.

Because the Old Testament rabbis could not see the gap between the first and second comings of the Messiah, some theorized that there would be two Messiahs— a "Messiah ben Joseph" who would suffer and a "Messiah ben David" who would conquer. From our New Testament perspective we can see that the Old Testament prophets were speaking of one Messiah who would come twice. We can see the gap between the two comings.

A Challenge

i ask you: How do you treat Zechariah 14—as fact or fiction? Are you guilty of playing games with God's Word in order to justify sacred traditions and doctrines of men?

I challenge you to interpret God's Word—all of it— for its plain-sense meaning. As you do so, you are very likely to find yourself challenged to discard old doctrines and to adopt new ones. This will be a painful process, but it will be a fruitful one, for you will be blessed with the truth of God's Word.

> If you abide in My word, then you are truly disciples of Mine; and you shall know the truth, and the truth shall make you free (John 8:31-32).

5

The Messiah in Prophecy

Does Prophecy Validate Jesus?

Was Jesus who He said He was? Was He really God in the flesh? Bible prophecy offers some of the strongest proof I know of that Jesus truly was divine.

Hundreds of Prophecies

The Old Testament contains more than 300 prophecies concerning the First Coming of Jesus. Some of these are repetitious, but when the repetition is accounted for, we are still left with at least 108 separate and distinct prophecies (see Appendix 1).

In addition to these explicit prophecies, there are many more symbolic prophecies which point to various aspects of the First Coming.

The book of Ruth, for example, does not contain any specific messianic prophecies. Yet the book's story contains a beautiful prophetic type of Jesus. One of the central characters, Boaz, is a kinsman-redeemer who takes a Gentile bride—just as Jesus came as a redeemer to His people, the Jews, and is now taking a Gentile bride, the Church.

The lives of Joshua, Jeremiah, and Daniel all give us insights into the faith, courage, and righteousness of the Messiah. Joshua and Jesus even had the same name, *Yeshua,* meaning "the salvation of God."

The life of Moses is a preview of many aspects of the life of Jesus. Moses tried to deliver his people from captivity and was rejected. In like manner, Jesus came to deliver His people from their spiritual bondage and was rejected by them. After his rejection, Moses took a Gentile bride. He then returned and was received by his people as a deliverer. Jesus is now taking a Gentile bride, the Church, and when He has completed that task, He will return and be received as Messiah by His own people, the Jews (Zechariah 12:10).

Every aspect of the life of Jesus was prophesied hundreds of years before He was born—the nature and place of His ministry, the nature of His death, and the triumph of His resurrection.

The very first prophecy in the Bible predicts that the Messiah will be born to a virgin. In Genesis 3:15 God says that the seed of the serpent will be defeated by the seed of the woman.

Genealogy in Prophecy

The entire lineage of the Messiah is prophesied in the Hebrew Scriptures. The prophets said the Savior would be born of the descendants of Abraham (Genesis 12:3), the heritage of Isaac (Genesis 17: 21), the children of Jacob (Genesis 28:14), the tribe of Judah (Genesis 49:8), the family of Jesse (Isaiah 11:1), and the house of David (Jeremiah 23:5).

That's why the Gospel of Matthew begins with such a long listing of Jesus' family tree. Matthew is trying to show His Jewish readers that the lineage of Jesus fulfills the predictions of the prophets.

Prophecy or Coincidence?

Some people shrug their shoulders at all these prophecies and say, "It's all a coincidence." Coincidence? The fulfillment of more than 100 prophecies?

"Well, He purposefully fulfilled them," says another. It is true that Jesus could have consciously fulfilled *some* of the prophecies about the Messiah. In fact, on one occasion it appears that Jesus did just that when He requested a donkey for His final ride into Jerusalem. Matthew says this was done to fulfill Zechariah's prophecy that the Messiah would come humbly, riding a donkey (Matthew 21:1-7).

But can a man purposefully fulfill prophecies concerning both his birth and death?

Micah prophesied 700 years before Jesus that the Messiah would be born in the little town of Bethlehem (Micah 5:2). Isaiah foretold that He would be born of a virgin (Isaiah 7:14). And Hosea said the Messiah would come out of Egypt (Hosea 11:1), the exact place the parents of Jesus took Him to after His birth.

Jesus was betrayed for 30 pieces of silver. The prophet Zechariah made that precise prophecy 500 years before Jesus was born! (See Zechariah 11:13.) David foresaw that the Messiah would be crucified (Psalm 22:16), and that was 1,000 years before the birth of Jesus and 700 years before the extensive use of crucifixion by the Romans.

How could Jesus fulfill these prophecies purposefully? And could their fulfillment be just a "coincidence"?

Prophecy and Mathematics

Peter Stoner, in his book *Science Speaks,* has calculated the odds that just eight of the prophecies concerning

Jesus could have been fulfilled accidentally in the life of one man. The odds are one in ten to the seventeenth power! That's the number 10 with 17 zeros after it!

To illustrate these mathematical odds, Stoner asks us to imagine filling the state of Texas knee-deep with silver dollars. A plane flies over and one silver dollar is dropped with a black checkmark on it. Bulldozers move in and mix the silver dollars thoroughly for a couple of years. A man is then blindfolded and turned loose in this sea of silver dollars.

The odds that he would reach down and pick up the marked silver dollar on the first draw are the same as eight of the Bible's prophecies about the Messiah being fulfilled in the life of one man accidentally. You might as well argue that a Boeing 747 could be the accidental product of a tornado blowing through a junkyard!

Prophecy as Proof

The powerful testimony of fulfilled prophecy in the life of Jesus is the reason that the Gospel writers constantly appeal to it in their writings to prove that Jesus was the promised Messiah. It is the reason Jesus appealed to it in His teachings to the masses (Matthew 5:17-18). It's also the reason Jesus emphasized it in His postresurrection teachings to His disciples (Luke 24:25ff).

Likewise, the apostles constantly cited prophetic fulfillment in their sermons to verify the identity of Jesus. On the Day of Pentecost, Peter focused his remarks in that first gospel sermon on the prophecies of David which Jesus had fulfilled (Acts 2:24-36). Peter utilized prophecy again in his second sermon at the Temple (Acts 3:12-26) and in his sermon to Cornelius and his household (Acts 10).

In his first epistle, Peter refers to three cardinal evidences of the deity of Jesus. He first mentions that he was an "eyewitness of His majesty"—a reference to the

Transfiguration. Then he mentions that he heard an "utterance made from heaven" in which God the Father proclaimed Jesus as His "beloved Son." Finally, he appeals to the testimony of prophecy, pointing to its fulfillment in the life of Jesus (2 Peter 1:16-19).

Philip used a prophecy from Isaiah to convert the Ethiopian eunuch (Acts 8). Paul also referred constantly to fulfilled prophecy in his preaching of the gospel (Acts 17:2-3). In fact, when Paul wrote his famous definition of the gospel in 1 Corinthians 15, he stressed that all the major events in the life of Jesus had happened "according to the Scriptures" (1 Corinthians 15:4).

Some Questions

How do you feel about the evidence of Bible prophecy? Are you going to try to explain it away? Are you going to write it off to "coincidence"? Are you simply going to ignore it?

God is not calling you to a blind faith based upon no evidence. Prophecy is *evidence*. It is evidence that demands a verdict. What is your verdict?

I believe fulfilled prophecy proves that Jesus was who He said He was.

Fulfilled prophecy also proves that the last prophecy of the Bible, a prophecy yet to be fulfilled, is one we can rely upon. It is contained in Revelation 22:20 and it was spoken by Jesus Himself: "Surely I am coming soon" (RSVB).

Amen. Come, Lord Jesus!

6

Prophecy and Salvation

Is Millennial Belief Essential?

What is the relationship of prophetic doctrine to salvation? Is it possible to be saved and yet reject the biblical teaching that the Lord is going to return and reign over all the world for a thousand years?

I raise this issue because differences in prophetic doctrine have been used by many denominational groups to draw lines of fellowship between Christians. Some have even gone so far as to make prophetic doctrine a condition of salvation!

A Personal Experience

I speak from painful personal experience regarding this point. I grew up in a denomination that was amillennial in its prophetic viewpoint. That means we rejected completely the idea that Jesus would ever return to this earth to reign.

Our church leaders felt so strongly about this issue that they made it a test of fellowship and a condition of salvation. Any person among us who developed a premillennial view (that Jesus would return to reign for a thousand years) was labeled "heretical" and was sooner or later (usually sooner) given the left foot of fellowship. They would then write off that person as one who had "fallen from grace."

I eventually became one of those brothers who was condemned and shunned because my study of the Word led me to adopt a premillennial interpretation of prophecy.

The Problem

The fundamental problem here has nothing whatsoever to do with prophecy. The problem is the erroneous concept of salvation.

Those who draw lines of fellowship over matters like prophetic interpretation are people who believe in salvation by perfected knowledge; that is, they believe that salvation is dependent upon being right about every doctrine.

I can still vividly recall a classic expression of this attitude several years ago at a prophecy conference I helped put together. We tried to arrange to have a speaker representing each of the major prophetic viewpoints.

The person who presented the amillennial view, a preacher from my childhood denomination, was asked after his presentation whether or not a premillennialist could be saved. His response was, "I couldn't be saved if I were premillennialist, because I know it's wrong." I wanted to jump up and stop the discussion on prophecy and spend the rest of the day discussing the real issue of salvation.

Are we saved by being right about prophecy? Can I really lose my salvation if I am wrong about my belief that Jesus is coming back to reign upon the earth?

If you and I can be lost by being wrong about prophecy, then we can be lost by being wrong about anything—such as the frequency of communion or the role of women in the Church. That means we really have no hope of salvation because none of us is right about everything.

The Certainty of Salvation

And yet the Bible says we can be confident of our salvation. Consider these words of the apostle John:

> We know that we have passed out of death into life (1 John 3:14).

> These things I have written to you who believe in the name of the Son of God, in order that you may know that you have eternal life (1 John 5:13).

> We know that we are of God (1 John 5:19).

Over and over John says we can know that we are saved.

But how can we ever have such assurance if our salvation depends upon our being right about everything? The answer is that we can't. And that is precisely why some conservative churches are filled with souls who seem sure of everything except the most important thing of all—namely, their salvation!

You can know with absolute certainty that you are saved because Paul said you are saved by the grace of God, "as a gift" (Romans 3:24). You can also be certain about your salvation, because if you are saved, then you know your Savior, and you know He is trustworthy and that He meant it when He said, "I am the resurrection and the life; he who believes in Me shall live even if he dies" (John 11:25).

Our confidence is also assured by Paul's glorious proclamation, "There is therefore now no condemnation for those who are in Christ Jesus" (Romans 8:1).

The Essence of Salvation

This means that you and I can be wrong about a lot of things, but if we are right about one thing—Jesus Christ—then we can claim the promise of eternal salvation. All truth is important, but it is not all equally important.

Accordingly, whatever the truth may be about such things as instrumental music or communion or prophecy, these truths are as nothing compared to *the* truth that Jesus is Lord (1 Corinthians 12:3). That's why Paul wrote, "If you confess with your mouth Jesus as Lord, and believe in your heart that God raised Him from the dead, you shall be saved" (Romans 10:9).

The essence of salvation is not doctrinal perfection. Rather, it is a relationship with a Person. Jesus put it this way: "This is eternal life, that they may know Thee, the only true God, and Jesus Christ whom Thou hast sent" (John 17:3).

Does this mean that what you believe about prophecy is irrelevant? Not at all! It just means that it has nothing to do with your justification—that is, with your judicial standing before God. We are justified by our faith in Jesus as our Lord and Savior (Romans 3:21-26).

The Process of Salvation

Much of the problem here is caused by a failure to distinguish between justification, sanctification, and glorification. The result is that many Christians are ignorant of the fact that salvation is a process.

Justification is the starting point. It occurs when you put your faith in Jesus.

The salvation process continues with your sanctification. This is a lifelong process of dying to self and living more and more for Christ.

The process consummates in your glorification, when you are resurrected and given an immortal body. It is then that you will stand face-to-face with the Lord and be fully conformed to His image (Romans 8:29-30).

Justification results in your adoption into the family of God. When you are justified, you put on the righteousness of Christ, and you stand guiltless before the judgment bar of God, washed clean in the blood of the Lamb (1 Corinthians 1:30). You receive the gift of the indwelling Holy Spirit as the guarantee of your eternal inheritance (Ephesians 1:13-14), and you begin your walk with the Lord.

The Meaning of Sanctification

It is true that you are sanctified when you are justified, because you are washed clean of your sins and are set apart from the world as God's sacred possession (1 Corinthians 6:11 and Hebrews 10:10). But the process of sanctification continues as you begin walking with the Lord.

Through the process of sanctification, God shapes your soul (your will, emotions, and personality) into the image of Christ. This takes place as you learn more and more about the Lord and His Word through Bible study, prayer, worship, and fellowship. This does not mean that sanctification is something you earn. Like justification, sanctification is a gift of God's grace through the power of His Holy Spirit working within you.

But whereas you are *justified* by responding to the truth of the gospel (the death, burial, and resurrection of Jesus—1 Corinthians 15:1-4), you are *sanctified* by responding to the truths of Christian doctrine. This means that the quality of your walk with the Lord will be substantially affected by what you believe about such things as the Holy Spirit, the Church, discipleship, stewardship, miracles, prayer, and prophecy.

The Impact of Prophecy

Before I came to a premillennial understanding of prophecy, I had little enthusiasm for the return of Christ. I certainly was not watchful for His return, and I felt that the only impact of His return on world history would be to bring it to an end.

Now I have a whole new perspective that has drawn me closer to the Lord and has strengthened my faith, deepened my love, and enhanced my hope.

I now look for the return of Christ with fervent expectancy as my "blessed hope" (Titus 2:13). My watchfulness has become a powerful motivator for holy living (Romans 13:11-14). I thrill to the thought of the triumph of Jesus over Satan (Revelation 20:1-2,10). I look forward with joy to the establishment of the Lord's reign of perfect peace and righteousness here on earth (Micah 4:1-7). I rejoice that Jesus will soon be fully vindicated in history, just as He was humiliated in history (Isaiah 24:21-23).

I have been brought to the awe-inspiring realization that one of the greatest miracles of history is occurring before my very eyes—the regathering of the Jews (Jeremiah 16:14-15). Scripture passages concerning the Jews which never had any meaning at all to me have suddenly come alive (Jeremiah 23:5-8; Ezekiel 36 and 37; Amos 9:14-15). For the first time I understand the meaning of Paul's writings in Romans 9-11, where he talks of God's grace for the Jewish people. I rejoice that a remnant of the Jews will come to know their Messiah (Zechariah 12:10) and that they will be established as the prime nation of the world through whom all the nations will be blessed (Isaiah 60-62).

I praise God for the redemption that Jesus will bring to all the creation (Romans 8:18-23). And I look forward with great anticipation to an eternity in the presence of God upon a New Earth that has been purged of its corruption and renovated to its previous glory (2 Peter 3:1-13 and Revelation 21:1-4).

I have a grasp of God's master plan of history that I never had before, and that has given me a sense of comfort and peace that serves as a sturdy anchor in such perilous times as these. I now know with certainty that God's Word is sure, that His promises are certain, that He is alive and well, that He still cares intensely about His creation, and that He still intervenes in marvelous and miraculous ways to direct and comfort His people while He orchestrates the evil deeds of Man to a climax that will bring eternal honor and glory to His holy name (Psalm 2).

A Call to Love

As you can see, what we believe about prophecy does make a difference in the quality of our Christian lives. That's why I always get a little annoyed when I hear a Christian saying, "I don't know anything about Bible prophecy, and I don't care, because what you believe about prophecy makes no difference." Not so. It makes a lot of difference.

Yet it should make no difference at all in our attitude toward each other as brothers and sisters in Christ. I have Christian brothers and sisters who are premillennialists and amillennialists and postmillennialists, and I have some relatives in Christ who don't know the difference between a millennium and a millipede! I will spend eternity with some who have never even read the book of Revelation.

We need to stop playing God by drawing lines of fellowship which we have no right to draw over matters of opinion, and we need to start loving each other because we share a belief in the fundamental fact of history that Jesus is Lord.

PART
2

Prophetic Issues

The prophecies are "things
into which angels long to look."
—1 Peter 1:10-12

7

The Jews
in Prophecy

Cast Aside or Destined for Glory?

Few biblical studies are as exciting as an examination of the Jews in prophecy, for the Jews are one of the key focal points of Bible prophecy.

The Scriptures reveal the Jews as "the apple of [God's] eye" (Zechariah 2:8). Their land is described as "holy" (Zechariah 2:12). Their city of Jerusalem is termed the "center of the nations" (Ezekiel 5:5). They are pictured as the wayward wife of God (see Ezekiel 16 and the book of Hosea). And the Bible makes it clear that they will be the object of both God's wrath (Jeremiah 30:7) and His grace (Zechariah 13:1) in the end times.

The panorama of prophecy that relates to the Jews is breathtaking. It applies to the past, the present, and the future. It demonstrates God's love and grace as nothing else does except the Cross itself.

Paul was so overwhelmed by God's patient determination to bring a remnant of the Jews to salvation that he cried out in ecstasy: "Oh, the depth of the riches both of the wisdom and knowledge of God! How unsearchable are His judgments and unfathomable His ways!" (Romans 11:33).

Let's take a look at the incredible prophecies that pertain to the Jewish people, and let's begin with the prophecies that have already been fulfilled.

Fulfilled Prophecies

1. *Dispersion*—The Jews were warned repeatedly that they would be dispersed worldwide if they were not faithful to their covenant with God. Consider the words of Moses: "The LORD will scatter you among all peoples, from one end of the earth to the other" (Deuteronomy 28:64; see also Leviticus 26:33).

2. *Persecution*—The Lord also warned the Jews that they would be persecuted wherever they went. Again, the words of Moses are graphic in this regard: "Among those nations you shall find no rest, and there shall be no resting place for the sole of your foot; but there the LORD will give you a trembling heart, failing of eyes, and despair of soul" (Deuteronomy 28:65).

3. *Desolation*—God promised that after their dispersion, their land would become "desolate" and their cities would become "waste" (Leviticus 26:33). Moses put it even more graphically when he said, "The foreigner who comes from a distant land ... will say, 'All its land is brimstone and salt, a burning waste, unsown and unproductive, and no grass grows in it'" (Deuteronomy 29:22-23).

4. *Preservation*—Yet God in His marvelous grace promised He would preserve the Jews as a separate people during their worldwide wanderings. (See Isaiah 66:22; Jeremiah 30:11; 31:35-37.) Isaiah puts it in a

colorful way. He says the Lord could no more forget Israel than a mother could forget her nursing child (Isaiah 49:15). He then adds that God cannot forget Israel because He has them tattooed on the palms of His hands (Isaiah 49:16)!

God has fulfilled all four of these prophecies during the past 2,000 years. In A.D. 70 the Romans destroyed the city of Jerusalem and took the Jewish nation into captivity, desolating the land and scattering the Jewish people across the face of the earth. As prophesied, everywhere they went they were persecuted, with their persecution culminating in the Nazi Holocaust of World War II.

But God also preserved the Jews, and the fulfillment of this prophecy has been one of the most remarkable miracles of history. No other people have ever been so dispersed and yet been able to retain their identity as a nation.

Current Prophecies

We are privileged to live in an age when God is fulfilling many promises to the Jews. What a testimony this is to the fact that God is alive and well, that God is on His throne and in control, and that God is faithful to His promises.

1. *Regathering*—The Old Testament prophets promise repeatedly that the day will come when God will regather the Jews to Palestine (see Isaiah 11:10-12 and Ezekiel 36:22-28). This remarkable regathering of the Jews from the four corners of the earth has occurred in our lifetime. World War I prepared the land for the people as the control of Palestine was transferred from a nation that hated the Jews (the Turks) to a nation that was sympathetic to their return (Britain). The Holocaust of World War II prepared the people for the land by motivating them to return.

2. *Nationhood*—The prophets stated that when the people were regathered, the nation of Israel would be re-established. This occurred on May 14, 1948 (see Isaiah 66:7-8; Zechariah 12:3-6). This is the cornerstone prophetic event of our age. It is an event that prophetic scholars have pointed to for 400 years amid much scoffing and ridicule by those who did not believe that Israel would ever exist again as a nation.

3. *Reclamation*—God promised that with the re-establishment of the nation, the land would bloom again (Isaiah 35:1-7; Joel 2:21-26). As Ezekiel put it, people would one day exclaim, "This desolate land has become like the garden of Eden" (Ezekiel 36:35). And that is exactly what people exclaim today when they visit Israel, for it is once again a land of milk and honey. Over 300 million trees have been planted in this century. Rainfall has increased 450 percent. The former malaria-infested swamps have been converted into cultivated land. Water from the Sea of Galilee has been channeled to the deserts, causing them to bloom.

4. *Language*—When the Jews were scattered world-wide in the first century, they ceased speaking the Hebrew language. The Jews who settled in Europe developed a language called Yiddish (a combination of Hebrew and German). The Jews in the Mediterranean basin mixed Hebrew with Spanish to produce a language called Ladino. The prophet Zephaniah implied a time would come when the Hebrew language would be revived (Zephaniah 3:9). It has been. Today the Israelis speak biblical Hebrew. It is the only example in history of the resurrection of a dead language. The man God used to revive the language was Eliezer Ben Yehuda (1858-1922).

5. *Jerusalem*—Jesus said that one of the surest signs of His imminent return would be the reoccupation of Jerusalem by the Jews (Luke 21:24). This occurred during the Six-Day War in June 1967.

6. *Military Strength*—Zechariah prophesied that when the Jews were reestablished in the land, their military strength would be overwhelming—like "a flaming torch among sheaves"—and that they would "consume" all the peoples around them (Zechariah 12:6). Need anything be said about the fulfillment of this prophecy?

7. *Focal Point*—Israel is always pictured as the focal point of world politics in the end times (Zechariah 12:3; 14:1-9). This has been true since the Arab oil boycott in 1973. The West suddenly realized its dependence on Arab oil and began to line up behind the Arab obsession to annihilate Israel.

Future Prophecies

1. *Tribulation*—God will put the Jewish people through an unparalleled period of tribulation (Deuteronomy 4:30) during which two-thirds of the Jews will perish (Zechariah 13:8-9). The purpose will be to soften the hearts of a remnant so that they will accept Jesus as their Messiah.

2. *Salvation*—A remnant of the Jews will "look on [Him] whom they have pierced" and will accept Him as Lord and Savior (Zechariah 12:10; Romans 11:1-6, 25-29).

3. *Primacy*—God will then regather all the believing Jews to Israel, where they will be established as the prime nation in the world during the Millennial Reign of Jesus. (See Deuteronomy 28:1,13; 2 Samuel 7:9; Isaiah 60-62; Micah 4:1-7.)

God's Infinite Love

God set the Jews aside and put them under discipline because of their disobedience, but He did not cut them off from His grace.

He intends to bring His wayward wife home: "The sons of Israel will remain for many days without king or

prince.... Afterward the sons of Israel will return and
seek the LORD their God... and they will come trembling to the LORD and to His goodness in the last days"
(Hosea 3:4-5).

The lovingkindness and faithfulness of God in keep-
ing His promises to the Jewish people should be a source
of encouragement to all Christians. As we watch God
fulfill promises which He made to the Jewish people
thousands of years ago, we can be absolutely certain
that He will be faithful to fulfill all the promises He has
made to the Church.

God's Amazing Grace

The first time my wife heard me preach about the
Jews in prophecy, she said, "When you talk about how
much God loves the Jews, you make me want to be one."

I responded, "No, Honey, you don't want to be a Jew
because if you were, you would likely have a veil over
your heart and would refuse to believe in Jesus as your
Messiah" (see 2 Corinthians 3:12-18).

I then stressed a point I hope you will never forget. I
emphasized that everything God is doing for the Jews
He is willing to do for you and me. They are witnesses of
His amazing grace and that same grace is available to
all of us, whether we be Gentiles or Jews.

8

The Arabs
in Prophecy

Fated for Hope or Despair?

The Arab peoples often seem to be ignored in prophecy. This is so because the prophetic Scriptures focus on the Jewish people since they are the Chosen People of God. But this does not mean the Arabs are ignored.

Jewish Primacy

God chose the Jews to give the world the Scriptures, and it was through the Jews that He provided the Messiah.

The Jews also serve as God's prophetic time clock, for He points to future events in their history as the key to the timing of other important events. (For example, Jesus said that He would return at a time when Jerusalem is back in the hands of the Jews—see Luke 21:24.)

The Jews continue to serve today as a chosen witness of God's grace. This is manifested in their very existence, for what other god would have tolerated for so long a people so stubborn and rebellious?

The Bible says that the Jewish people will continue to serve as the Chosen People in the future, for when Jesus returns, a remnant of the Jews who have put their faith in Him will be established as the prime nation of the world (Isaiah 60-62). During the Lord's millennial reign, the Jewish nation will be a channel of blessings to the whole world (Zechariah 8:23).

Does this mean that God has no blessings for the multitudinous Arab peoples? Not at all. God has given them great blessings in the past, and He has great blessings reserved for them in the future.

Arab Identity

Before we look at those blessings, let's consider first the identity of the Arab peoples. Who are they?

A popular misconception is that Arab identity is determined by religion—that if you are a Muslim, then you are an Arab. That is not true.

One of the most populous Muslim nations in the world is Indonesia, an island nation in Southeast Asia. Indonesians are not Arabs. They are Malays. Likewise, the nation of Iran is composed of Muslims, but they are not Arabs. They are Persians.

There are also Christian Arabs scattered all across the Middle East. In Israel, the city of Bethlehem is a Christian Arab town.

Arab identity is not determined by religion. Most Arabs are Muslims, but not all; and all Muslims are certainly not Arabs.

Arab identity is determined by ethnic heritage. And the amazing thing is that all Arabs—like all Jews—are descendants from the family of Abraham! That means the Arab-Israeli conflict is a family dispute—the longest-running and most intense family squabble in history.

Arab Origins

It all began when Abraham decided to help God. That's a nice way of saying that he decided to run ahead of God. I'm referring, of course, to his impatience with God's promise that he would be given an heir.

As he and Sarah continued to advance in years without a child, they decided to help out God by having Abraham conceive a child through Hagar, his wife's Egyptian handmaid. The child born of that union was named Ishmael. God made it clear that Ishmael would not be the child of promise through whom all the world would be blessed (Genesis 17:20-21), but God did make some great promises to Ishmael's mother.

God promised that He would make Ishmael fruitful and would multiply his descendants exceedingly, making of him a "great nation" (Genesis 17:20). He also gave Ishmael's descendants the land to the east of Canaan (Genesis 16:12).

God has been faithful to these promises. Today there are 21 Arab nations with a combined population of 175 million people. The Arabs occupy a total area of 5.3 million square miles of oil-rich land.

By contrast, there is only one Jewish state with a population of 4 million people who are squeezed into only 8,000 square miles of space. That's a population ratio of 43 to 1 and a land ratio of 662 to 1. The Arabs have truly been blessed.

Arab Tribes

Ishmael took an Egyptian wife (Genesis 21:21) and became the father of 12 tribes which are listed in Genesis 25:12-16. These tribes were to become the nucleus of the Arab peoples, a people with a mixture of Semitic and Egyptian blood.

Other Arab tribes trace their origin to the six sons of Abraham who were born to him by his second wife,

Keturah. They are listed in Genesis 25:1-4. Finally, some Arab tribes were to emerge from the descendants of Esau, the twin brother of Jacob, who sired the 12 tribes of Israel.

All the Arab tribes have been characterized historically by their impulsive and violent nature. They have been involved in endless wars among themselves and against both Jews and Christians.

It is interesting to note that their volatile nature is a fulfillment of prophecy. God told Hagar that her son, Ishmael, would be "a wild donkey of a man" and that "his hand will be against everyone" (Genesis 16:12).

Arab Prophecies

Now let's look at what the Bible prophesies about the Arab peoples. First, it says they will claim the land of Israel which God gave to their brothers, the Jews. The prophet Ezekiel says this claim will be made in the end times (Ezekiel 35:5,10; 36:2,5).

This prophecy has been fulfilled in this century. For 2,000 years the Jews were dispersed from the land which God gave them, and during that long period of time there was never an Arab state in the area that the world called Palestine. The Arabs who lived in the land considered themselves Syrians. They had no consciousness as Palestinians, and no effort was ever made to create a Palestinian state.

When the Jews began returning in this century, the Arabs gleefully sold them the land at inflated prices because it was considered worthless. It was World War I that changed the Arab viewpoint. The war resulted in the land of Palestine being transferred from the Turks to the British, and the British immediately proclaimed it to be a homeland for the Jews. Suddenly the Arabs were confronted with the prospect of a Jewish state, so they began to dig in their heels, claiming the land as their own.

The British gave in to Arab pressure, and in 1922 they gave two-thirds of Palestine to the Arabs, creating the state of Jordan. This was land that they had promised to the Jews. But this action did not satisfy the Arab appetite. They wanted all the land God had given to the Jews, and they still covet it to this day, just as prophesied.

Arab Judgments

The Bible further prophesies that God will pour out judgment upon the Arab nations in the end times for their hostility toward the Jews and their attempt to claim the Jewish homeland as their own.

Consider Joel 3:19, for example. This passage has a clear end-time context, and in that context it says, "Egypt will become a waste, and Edom will become a desolate wilderness, because of the violence done to the sons of Judah, in whose land they have shed innocent blood."

Keep in mind that "Edom" is often used as a symbolic term for all the Arab peoples, just as "Israel" is used as a term for all the Jewish tribes. Ezekiel says that "all Edom" will be dealt with in the end times because of its hatred against the Jews, and the result will be desolation (Ezekiel 35:10-11,15). The book of Obadiah prophesies a similar fate for Edom in "the day of the LORD" (Obadiah 15-18).

Arab Promises

But the future for the Arabs is not all bleak. They must suffer for their sins just as the Jewish people will suffer during the Tribulation. And, like the Jews, a remnant of the Arabs will emerge from their suffering with their hearts turned to the one and only true God (Jeremiah 12:14-17).

The most remarkable prophecy concerning the future salvation of an Arab remnant is contained in Isaiah 19:16-25. Isaiah says that when the Lord strikes

Egypt and Assyria, they will turn to Him and He will have compassion on them and "heal them." Isaiah then presents an incredible picture of Egypt, Assyria, and Israel living together in peace, worshiping the same God!

Another remarkable prophecy concerns the Arabs who will be living in the land of Israel after the Lord returns. This prophecy relates to the fact that the territory of Israel will be greatly expanded when Jesus returns, incorporating many of the Arab nations that exist today. (The considerably expanded borders of Israel during the Millennium are detailed in Ezekiel 47:15-20.) Amazingly, Ezekiel says that the Arabs living in Israel at that time will be "allotted an inheritance" of the land together with the tribes of Israel! (See Ezekiel 47:21-23 and Isaiah 14:1-2.)

An Impartial God

There is no partiality with God (Romans 2:11). He chose the Jews not to be a *repository* of His blessings, but to be a *vehicle* through whom He would bless *all* the nations of the world, including the Arabs. But the fundamental requirement to receive God's blessings—for both Jew and Arab, as well as all people—is to accept God's gift of love in Jesus by receiving Him as Messiah.

When I consider God's grace toward the Arab peoples, I am reminded of what Paul wrote when he considered God's grace toward his Jewish brethren: "Oh, the depth of the riches both of the wisdom and knowledge of God! How unsearchable are His judgments and unfathomable His ways!" (Romans 11:33).

Keep in mind that the amazing grace which God is displaying toward the Arabs and the Jews is available to you. The message of God's dealings with the physical descendants of Abraham is that there is no sin so great and dark that it can separate you from the love of God which He has expressed in Jesus.

9

The Gentiles in Prophecy

Spent Glory or Future Empire?

"Jerusalem will be trampled underfoot by the Gentiles until the times of the Gentiles be fulfilled."

—Luke 21:24

Although the Scriptures focus upon God's dealings with His Chosen People, the Jews, the non-Jews (known in the Bible as the Gentiles) are not ignored—as the above quote from Jesus demonstrates.

The Bible teaches that God chose the Jewish people to serve as witnesses of His glory (Isaiah 41:10-12). He also chose them to serve as a channel of His blessings to the world (Genesis 12:1-3).

Through the Jews, God revealed Himself and His Law. And through the Jewish prophets, He pointed Mankind to the coming Messiah (1 Peter 1:10-12).

The Focus Shifts

God did not start using the Gentiles as a vehicle of His purposes in history until His Chosen People turned their backs on Him and gave themselves to human idols. At that point in time, God began to work through both the Jews and the Gentiles to carry out His scheme of redemption.

His first step was to bring judgment upon the Jews for their idolatry. He did this by allowing them to be taken into exile by the Babylonians.

It was during this exile (about 600 B.C.) that God revealed to His prophet Daniel that He had a plan for using the Gentile nations to help achieve His purposes in history.

A Prophetic Dream

Daniel was one of the Jewish exiles. He came to the attention of the Babylonian leaders through his ability to interpret dreams. He was called upon to interpret a troubling dream which God gave to the Babylonian king, Nebuchadnezzar.

The king saw a huge statue of a man in his dream. The statue was made of a succession of metals. It had a head of gold, a silver chest, thighs of brass, and legs of iron. It rested upon a precarious foundation—feet of iron mixed with clay.

As Nebuchadnezzar stared at the statue, admiring its beauty, the feet were suddenly struck by a supernatural stone ("a stone . . . cut out without hands"). The statue collapsed and the stone expanded rapidly into a mountain that engulfed the whole world (Daniel 2:31-35).

Daniel explained that the dream dealt with the future and extended even to the "latter days" (Daniel 2:28). He pointed out that the golden head was representative of the Babylonian Empire. It would be succeeded by another empire represented by the silver chest, and that would, in turn, be overthrown by another empire symbolized by the thighs of bronze. The final empire was represented by the legs of iron (Daniel 2:36-40).

Later, God revealed to Daniel that the empire that would follow Babylon would be the Medo-Persian, which, in turn, would be overthrown by the Greeks under Alexander the Great (Daniel 8:1-8,20-21).

The empire represented by the iron legs was never specifically identified, but we know from history that it was the Roman Empire, which eventually split into two parts, the Eastern and Western Empires.

A Prophetic Gap

The prophecy evidently contains a time gap because there is nothing in history that corresponds to the empire represented by the feet of iron mixed with clay.

In subsequent dreams and visions, the Lord revealed to Daniel that this kingdom of iron mixed with clay would be a loose confederation of ten nations (Daniel 7:24). This confederation would arise out of the territory of the empire of iron—the Roman Empire (Daniel 7:7-8). Daniel was also shown that this revived European confederation would serve as the base for the construction of the last great Gentile world empire—namely, the empire of the Antichrist (Daniel 7:8,24-26; 8:19-27).

Further evidence of a time gap is found in the fact that history fails to show a ten-nation European confederation expanding into a world empire and then being suddenly destroyed by a supernatural intervention of God. Nor has a kingdom from God yet encompassed the whole world, submitting the nations to the rule of the Messiah (Daniel 2:41-45; 7:13-14,27).

A Prophetic Expectation

The "times of the Gentiles" began with Nebuchadnezzar. They continue to this day.

The ruthless glory of the Gentile empires came to an end when the Roman Empire split and then later collapsed. At that point the international community reorganized into nation-states.

But the glory is not all past. The greatest Gentile empire is still future. It will be the empire of the Antichrist.

That's what all the talk about a "New World Order" is all about. Satan is coalescing a new worldwide Gentile empire. Its nucleus is being provided through the reunification of Europe.

Before long, some dynamic, charismatic political personality will emerge in Europe who seems to have the answers to all the world's problems. Europe will unite behind him, and he will then venture forth to build a New World Order, using both deception and force (Daniel 11:36-45 and Revelation 6:1-6).

The final Gentile empire will unite the world politically, socially, economically, and spiritually. The Antichrist will be assisted by a False Prophet who will pull together the world's religions into an amalgamated, apostate superchurch that will worship the Antichrist (Revelation 13:11-18).

At the end of seven years of unparalleled tribulation upon the earth, God will pour out His wrath upon this last Gentile empire. Its overwhelming destruction by fire will take place in one hour (Revelation 18).

That's when Jesus will return to set up another New World Order—the perfect world order. He will reign from Mount Zion in Jerusalem with a rod of iron, and the world will be flooded with peace, righteousness, and justice (Psalm 2 and Micah 4).

Prophetic Urgency

The "times of the Gentiles" are rapidly coming to a close. Jesus said the final days of this time period would be marked by the liberation of Jerusalem from Gentile control (Luke 21:24). That glorious event took place on June 7, 1967, when the Jews reconquered the city of Jerusalem for the first time in 1,897 years.

The Church may not have understood the significance of this event, but the Orthodox Jews certainly did. Rabbi Shlomo Goren, the Chief Rabbi of the Israeli Army in 1967, rushed to the Wailing Wall, blew a shofar, and solemnly proclaimed "the beginning of the Messianic Age!"

The Orthodox Jews know the Old Testament prophecies, and those prophecies say that the Jews will be back in the land of Israel and the city of Jerusalem when the Messiah comes (Ezekiel 37).

A Warning

Do not be deceived by all the talk about a New World Order. It is the old world order dressed up in new clothes.

Satan is pulling together one last worldwide Gentile empire in his futile attempt to frustrate God's master plan. Most of the world will be deceived into believing that this New World Order will produce a utopia on earth. It will create, instead, a living hell.

The New World Order is doomed to failure, for it will be based on the wisdom of Man. Pray for the coming of the perfect world order that Jesus will establish when He returns. It will be based upon the Word of God.

10

The Church
in Prophecy

Tribulation or Heaven?

One of the hottest debates in prophecy today revolves around the question of whether the Church will go through the Tribulation or be taken to Heaven before it begins.

The concept that the Church will be taken out of the world before the Tribulation begins is called the "pre-Tribulation Rapture." It is a comforting thought, but is it biblical?

The Term

The term "rapture" comes from a Latin word that means to catch up, to snatch away, or to take out.

The word comes right out of the Latin Vulgate translation of 1 Thessalonians 4:17. In the New American Standard Version, the English phrase "caught up" is used. The same phrase is used in the King James and New International versions.

A Promise to the Church

The concept of the Rapture was not revealed to the Old Testament prophets because it is a promise to the New Testament Church and not to the saints of God who lived before the establishment of the Church.

The saints of Old Testament times will be resurrected at the end of the Tribulation and not at the time of the Rapture of the Church. Daniel reveals this fact in Daniel 12:1-2, where he says that the saints of that age will be resurrected at the end of the "time of distress."

Biblical References

The first clear mention of the Rapture in Scripture is found in the words of Jesus recorded in John 14:1-4. Jesus said, "I will come again, and receive you to Myself; that where I am, there you may be also."

The most detailed revelation of the actual events related to the Rapture is given by Paul in 1 Thessalonians 4:13-18. He says that when Jesus appears, the dead in Christ (Church-age saints) will be resurrected and caught up first. Then those of us who are alive in Christ will be translated "to meet the Lord in the air." Paul then exhorts us to "comfort one another with these words."

Paul mentions the Rapture again in 1 Corinthians 15—his famous chapter on the resurrection of the dead: "Behold, I tell you a mystery; we shall not all sleep, but we shall be changed, in a moment, in the twinkling of an eye, at the last trumpet" (verses 51 and 52).

Paul's reference here to being changed is an allusion to the fact that the saints will receive glorified bodies that will be perfected, imperishable, and immortal (1 Corinthians 15:42-44,50-55).

The Timing

The most controversial aspect of the Rapture is its timing. Some place it at the end of the Tribulation, making it one and the same event as the Second Coming. Others place it in the middle of the Tribulation. Still others believe that it will occur at the beginning of the Tribulation.

The reason for these differing viewpoints is that the exact time of the Rapture is not precisely revealed in Scripture. It is only implied. There is, therefore, room for honest differences of opinion, and lines of fellowship should certainly not be drawn over differences regarding this point, even though it is an important point.

Post-Tribulation Rapture

Those who place the timing at the end of the Tribulation usually base their argument on two parables in Matthew 13 and on the Lord's Olivet Discourse in Matthew 24.

In Matthew 24 the Lord portrays His gathering of the saints as an event that will take place "immediately after the tribulation of those days" (Matthew 24:29). This certainly sounds like a post-Tribulation Rapture. But it must be kept in mind that the book of Matthew was written to the Jews, and therefore the recording of Jesus' speech by Matthew has a distinctively Jewish flavor to it as compared to Luke's record of the same speech.

Note, for example, Matthew's references to Judea and to Jewish law regarding travel on the Sabbath (Matthew 24:15-20). These are omitted in Luke's account. Instead, Luke speaks of the saints looking up for deliverance "to escape all these things" (Luke 21:36) when the end-time signs "begin to take place" (Luke 21:28). The saints in Matthew are instructed to flee from Judea and hide. The saints in Luke are told to look up for deliverance.

It appears, therefore, that Matthew and Luke are speaking of two different sets of saints. The saints in Matthew's account are most likely Jews who receive Jesus as their Messiah during the Tribulation. The saints in Luke are those who receive Christ before the Tribulation begins. Most of those who accept the Lord during the Tribulation will be martyred (Revelation 7:9-14). Those who live to the end will be gathered by the angels of the Lord (Matthew 24:31).

The parable of the wheat and tares (Matthew 13:24-30) and the parable of the dragnet (Matthew 13:47-50) can be explained in the same way. They refer to a separation of saints and sinners that will take place at the end of the Tribulation. The saints are those who receive Jesus as their Savior during the Tribulation (Gentile and Jew) and who live to the end of that awful period.

Mid-Tribulation Rapture

There are variations of the mid-Tribulation Rapture concept. The most common is that the Church will be taken out in the exact middle of the Tribulation, at the point in time when the Antichrist is revealed.

This concept is based upon a statement in 1 Corinthians 15:52, which says that the Rapture will occur at the blowing of "the last trumpet." Mid-Tribulation supporters identify this trumpet with the seventh trumpet of the trumpet judgments in the book of Revelation. Since the blowing of the seventh trumpet is recorded in Revelation 11, the midpoint of the Tribulation, the conclusion is that the Rapture must occur in the middle of the Tribulation.

But there are two problems with this interpretation. The first is that the last trumpet of 1 Corinthians 15 is blown for *believers*, whereas the seven trumpets of Revelation 8, 9, and 11 are sounded for *unbelievers*. The Revelation trumpets have no relevance for the Church. The last trumpet of 1 Corinthians 15 is a trumpet for the *righteous*. The last trumpet for the *unrighteous* is the one described in Revelation 11.

Another problem with this interpretation is that the passage in Revelation 11 that portrays the sounding of the seventh trumpet is a "flash-forward" to the end of the Tribulation. Flash-forwards are very common in the book of Revelation. They occur after something terrible is described in order to assure the reader that everything is going to turn out all right when Jesus returns at the end of the Tribulation.

Thus, the eighth and ninth chapters of Revelation, which describe the horrors of the trumpet judgments, are followed immediately by a flash-forward in chapter 10 that pictures the return of Jesus in victory at the end of the Tribulation. The mid-Tribulation action resumes in chapter 11 with a description of the killing of the two great prophets of God by the Antichrist. Then, to offset that terrible event, we are presented with another flash-forward, beginning with verse 15. The seventh trumpet is sounded and we find ourselves propelled forward to the end of the Tribulation when "the kingdom of the world has become the kingdom of our Lord."

The point is that the seventh trumpet of Revelation relates to the end of the Tribulation and not the middle. It is therefore no basis for an argument in behalf of a mid-Tribulation Rapture.

Pre-Wrath Rapture

A variation of the mid-Tribulation Rapture is the pre-wrath Rapture concept, which places the Rapture at the beginning of the last quarter of the Tribulation, about five-and-a-half years into the Tribulation.

The argument for this view is that the Church is promised protection only from the wrath of God and not the wrath of Man or of Satan. It is then argued that only the bowl judgments in the last quarter of the Tribulation (Revelation 16) represent the wrath of God.

But the argument for this view disintegrates when you consider two facts. First, it is Jesus Himself who breaks the seals that launch each of the seal judgments recorded in Revelation 6. These judgments occur at the beginning of the Tribulation. Second, the seven angels who blow the trumpets that initiate each of the trumpet judgments are given their trumpets at the throne of God (Revelation 8:2).

All the judgments of Revelation are clearly superintended by God. That is the reason we are told in Revelation 15:1 that the bowl judgments at the end of the Tribulation will *finish* the wrath of God, not *begin* His wrath.

The Pre-Tribulation Rapture

I believe the best inference of Scripture is that the Rapture will occur at the beginning of the Tribulation. The most important reason I believe this has to do with the issue of imminence. Over and over in Scripture we are told to watch for the appearing of the Lord. We are told to "be ready" (Matthew 24:44), to "be on the alert" (Matthew 24:42), to "be dressed in readiness" (Luke 12:35), and to "keep your lamps alight" (Luke 12:35). The clear force of these persistent warnings is that Jesus can appear at any moment.

Only the pre-Tribulation concept of the Rapture allows for the imminence of the Lord's appearing for His Church. When the Rapture is placed at any other point in time, the imminence of the Lord's appearing is destroyed because other prophetic events must happen first.

For example, if the Rapture is going to occur in mid-Tribulation, then why should I live looking for the Lord's appearing at any moment? I would be looking instead for an Israeli peace treaty, the rebuilding of the Temple, and the revelation of the Antichrist. Then and only then could the Lord appear.

The Focus of Attention

This raises the issue of what we are to be looking for. Nowhere are believers told to watch for the appearance of the Antichrist. On the contrary, we are told to watch for Jesus Christ. In Titus 2:13 Paul says we are to live "looking for the blessed hope and the appearing of the glory of our great God and Savior, Christ Jesus." Likewise, Peter urges us to "fix your hope completely on the grace to be brought to you at the revelation of Jesus Christ" (1 Peter 1:13). John completes the apostolic chorus by similarly urging us to fix our hope on Jesus at His appearing (1 John 3:2-3).

Only Matthew speaks of watching for the Antichrist (Matthew 24:15), but he is speaking to the Jews living in Israel in the middle of the Tribulation when the Antichrist desecrates the rebuilt Temple.

The Promise of Deliverance

Another argument in behalf of a pre-Tribulation Rapture has to do with the promises of God to protect the Church from His wrath. As has already been demonstrated, the book of Revelation shows that the wrath of God will be poured out during the entire period of the Tribulation.

The Word promises over and over that the Church will be delivered from God's wrath. Romans 5:9 says that "we shall be saved from the wrath of God through Him [Jesus]." First Thessalonians 1:10 states that we are waiting "for His Son from heaven...who delivers us from the wrath to come." The promise is repeated in 1 Thessalonians 5:9: "God has not destined us for wrath, but for obtaining salvation through our Lord Jesus Christ."

Supernatural Protection?

Some argue that God could supernaturally protect the Church during the Tribulation. Yes, He could. In fact, He promises to do just that for the 144,000 Jews who will be sealed as bond-servants at the beginning of the Tribulation (Revelation 7:1-8).

But God's promise to the Church during the Tribulation is not one of *protection* but one of *deliverance*. Jesus said we would "escape" the horrors of the Tribulation (Luke 21:36). Paul says Jesus is coming to "deliver" us from God's wrath (1 Thessalonians 1:10). Likewise, Peter says that if God could rescue righteous Lot from Sodom and Gomorrah, then He "knows how to rescue the godly from trial" (2 Peter 2:6-9).

Escapism?

The pre-Tribulation concept of the Rapture has often been condemned as "escapism." I think this criticism is unjustied. The Bible itself says that Christians are to "comfort one another" with the concept of the Rapture (1 Thessalonians 4:18). Is it a comfort to think of the Rapture occurring at the end of the world's worst period of war instead of at the beginning?

Regardless of when the Rapture actually occurs, we need to keep in mind that the Bible teaches that societal conditions are going to grow increasingly worse the closer we get to the Lord's return. That means Christians will suffer tribulation whether or not they go into the Great Tribulation. And that means all of us had better be preparing ourselves for unprecedented suffering and spiritual warfare.

If you are a Christian, you can do this daily by putting on "the full armor of God" (Ephesians 6:13), praying at all times in the Spirit that you will be able to stand firm against the attacks of Satan (Ephesians 6:14-18).

If you are not a Christian, your only hope is to reach out in faith and receive the free gift of God's salvation, which He has provided through His Son, Jesus (John 3:16).

11

The Earth in Prophecy

Eternal Restoration or Fiery Finish?

Did you know we are living on earth number three? Did you know the Bible reveals that there are two earths yet to come? Did you know the Bible teaches that the earth is eternal?

Earth I

The first earth was the one created in the beginning (Genesis 1:1). It was perfect in every respect (Genesis 1:31). But because of Man's sin, God placed a curse upon the earth (Genesis 3:17-19).

The Bible indicates that this curse radically altered the nature of God's original creation. Instead of Man exercising dominion over Nature as originally planned (Genesis 1:26,28), Nature rose up in conflict with Man as poisonous plants, carnivorous animals, and climatic cataclysms (like tornadoes) suddenly appeared.

Earth II

The curse radically altered the original earth, but Earth II was still quite different from the one we live on today. There is much evidence in both Genesis and Job that the second earth had a thick vapor canopy which shielded life from the ultraviolet radiation of the sun (see Genesis 2:5-6 and Job 38:8-11), producing the long lifespans recorded in Genesis.

The whole earth was like a greenhouse with thick vegetation growing everywhere, even at the poles. There was also probably only one large land mass.

Once again the sinful rebellion of Mankind motivated God to change the nature of the earth (Genesis 6:11-13). The change agent this time was water. It appears that God caused the vapor canopy to collapse (Genesis 7:11). He also caused "fountains of the great deep" to break forth upon the surface of the earth (Genesis 7:11).

Earth III

Like the curse, the Flood radically altered the nature of the earth. It produced Earth III, the earth we now live on.

The earth tilted on its axis, forming the polar caps. The unified land mass was split apart, forming the continents as we now know them (which is why they fit together like a jigsaw puzzle—see Genesis 10:25). And the vapor canopy was so completely depleted that ultraviolet radiation began to reach the earth in unprecedented levels, resulting in greatly reduced lifespans, first to 120 years and then to 70 years.

The Bible reveals that the current earth, Earth III, will be radically changed again at the Second Advent of Jesus. The change agents will be earthquakes on the earth and supernatural phenomena in the heavens.

The changes produced will so totally alter the earth and its atmosphere that Isaiah refers to the "new heavens and new earth" which will exist during the reign of the Lord (Isaiah 65:17).

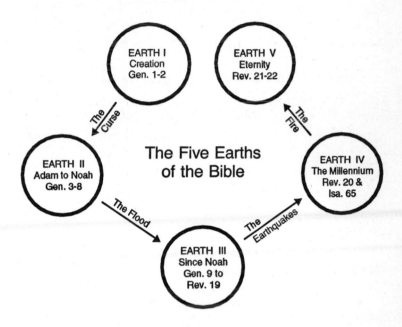

Figure 11-1: The Earth: Past, Present, and Future

Earth IV

Earth IV—the millennial earth—will be very different from the present earth. The earthquakes that will produce it will be the most severe in history.

Every valley will be lifted, every mountain will be lowered, and every island will be moved (Revelation 6:12-14; 16:17-21). Jerusalem will be lifted up, and Mount Zion will become the highest of all the mountains (Zechariah 14:10 and Micah 4:1).

The vapor canopy will likely be restored because life spans will be expanded to what they were at the beginning of time (Isaiah 65:20,22).

Further evidence that the vapor canopy will be restored is to be found in the fact that all the earth will become abundant once again with lush vegetation (Isaiah 30:23-26 and Amos 9:13-14). The Dead Sea will also become alive (Ezekiel 47:1-9).

Most important, the curse will be partially lifted, making it possible for Man to be reconciled to nature and for nature to be reconciled to itself. The wolf will dwell with the lamb because the wolf will no longer be carnivorous (Isaiah 11:6). The nursing child will play with the cobra because the cobra will no longer be poisonous (Isaiah 11:8).

Earth V

But Satan's last revolt at the end of the Millennium will leave the earth polluted and devastated (Revelation 20:7-9). Thus, at the end of the Lord's reign, God will take the Redeemed off the earth, place them in the New Jerusalem, and then cleanse the earth with fire (2 Peter 3:10-13).

In other words, God will superheat this earth in a fiery inferno and then reshape it like a hot ball of wax. The result will be the new heavens and new earth prophesied in Isaiah 66 and Revelation 21.

This will be Earth V, the perfected, eternal earth where the Redeemed will spend eternity in the New Jerusalem in the presence of God (Revelation 21:1-4). The curse will be completely lifted from this earth (Revelation 22:3).

> A generations goes and a generation comes, but the earth remains forever (Ecclesiastes 1:4).

Restoration in the Old Testament

God loves His creation, and He is determined to restore it to its original perfection.

This purpose of God was reflected in the rites of the Tabernacle of Moses. Each year when the High Priest entered the Holy of Holies to make atonement for the sins of the nation, he would sprinkle blood on the Mercy Seat of the Ark—and also on the ground in front of the Ark (Leviticus 16:15).

The blood on the Mercy Seat pointed to the promise of God that one day He would send a Messiah who would shed His blood so that the mercy of God could cover the Law and make it possible for us to be reconciled to our Creator. The blood on the ground pointed to the promise of God that the sacrifice of the Messiah would also make it possible for the creation to be redeemed.

In the Old Testament, Isaiah 11 gives us a beautiful picture of the redeemed creation during the Millennium. We are told that the meat-eating animals will cease to prey on each other and "will eat straw like the ox." The poisonous animals will also be transformed. They will cease to be dangerous (Isaiah 11:6-9; 35:9).

The plant kingdom will similarly be transformed back to its original perfection before the curse. The result will be incredible agricultural abundance:

> "Behold, days are coming," declares the LORD, "when the plowman will overtake the reaper and the treader of grapes him who sows seed; when the mountains will drip sweet wine" (Amos 9:13).

The prophet Joel adds that "the threshing floors will be full of grain, and the vats will overflow with the new wine and oil" (Joel 2:24).

The implication of these passages is that Man will no longer have to strive against nature because weeds and poisonous plants will cease to exist and rainfall will be abundant.

In fact, Isaiah tells us that areas of wilderness will be transformed into glorious forests (Isaiah 35:2) and deserts will become "springs of water" (Isaiah 35:7).

Restoration in the New Testament

The promise of a redeemed and restored creation is reaffirmed in the New Testament.

Peter referred to the promise in his second sermon at the Temple in Jerusalem. He told his audience that Jesus would remain in Heaven until the time comes for the "restoration of all things" (Acts 3:21).

Paul elaborates the theme in Romans 8:8-18. He declares that the whole creation is in "slavery to corruption" (verse 21). This is a reference to what physicists call the Second Law of Thermodynamics: All of creation is running down, moving from order to disorder; all of creation is in bondage to decay.

Paul then pictures the creation as a pregnant woman waiting anxiously for the moment of delivery when the curse will be lifted and the creation will be redeemed. He says that will occur at "the revealing of the sons of God" (verse 19).

That is a reference to the resurrection of the saints, a point he makes clear in verse 23 when he says that the saints should yearn with nature for that same event because that is when we will receive "the redemption of our body."

The Eternal Earth

The Old Testament has little to say about the eternal earth which God will create at the end of the Millennium. Isaiah simply asserts that such an earth will be provided (Isaiah 66:22). Isaiah's only other reference to a "new earth," in Isaiah 65:17, is a reference to the renovated earth of the Millennium.

In Revelation 21 the apostle John gives us the most detailed look at what the new, eternal earth will be like. And yet, his description is tantalizingly vague. He makes a cryptic reference to the fact that there will no longer be any sea (Revelation 21:1). Beyond that, all he tells us is that God will make "all things new" (Revelation 21:5).

Some believe the reference to the sea is symbolic since that word is often used in prophecy to refer to the Gentile nations (see Luke 21:25 and Revelation 13:1). They thus interpret this statement about the sea to mean that the nations will no longer be divided between and against each other.

Others interpret the reference literally and argue that it is a clue that there will be one land mass on the New Earth and that the seas will no longer separate peoples of the world as they do today.

The description of the New Jerusalem in Revelation 21 implies that the eternal earth will be much larger than the current earth. This inference is drawn from the fact that the New Jerusalem will be shaped as a 1,500-mile cube. Such a structure would be completely out of proportion to the size of the current earth.

A Glorious Blessing

I think the reason these passages about the eternal earth tell us so little about the features of that earth is because they focus on one glorious fact that overshadows any concern with what the New Earth will be like. The fact is that the Redeemed will live in the presence of Almighty God (Revelation 21 and 22). We will "serve Him" and we will "see His face" (Revelation 22:3-4). What the earth will be like pales in comparison to this revelation.

Are you an heir of this wonderful promise? The Bible says that "he who overcomes shall inherit these things" (Revelation 21:7).

Are you an overcomer? The Bible defines an overcomer in 1 John 5:1-5 as any person "who believes that Jesus is the Son of God." Such a person is portrayed as being "born of God."

12

Jerusalem in Prophecy

Insignificance or Glory?

Jerusalem is the most important city in the world, for it is "the city of our God" (Psalm 48:1,8). God loves it (Psalm 122), and He intends to dwell there when the eternal state begins (Psalm 68:16; 132:13-14).

It is no wonder that Jerusalem is identified in the Bible as being "the center of the nations" (Ezekiel 5:5) and "the center of the world" (Ezekiel 38:12).

Jerusalem is where Jesus shed His blood for the sins of Mankind. It is where Jesus will soon return to be crowned the King of kings. Ultimately, it is where God Himself will come to reside for all eternity (Ezekiel 43:7). For these reasons, Jerusalem has always been an important topic of Bible prophecy.

Gentile Jerusalem

During the last week of His life, Jesus prophesied that the city of Jerusalem would be totally destroyed

(Luke 21:5-6,20-24). "There will not be left one stone upon another which will not be torn down," Jesus said (Luke 21:6).

His prophecy was fulfilled 40 years later when the Romans under Titus destroyed the city, burned the Temple, and took the Jews into exile.

Jesus further prophesied that the city would suffer Gentile occupation for many years: "Jerusalem will be trampled under foot by the Gentiles until the times of the Gentiles be fulfilled" (Luke 21:24).

This prophecy has also been fulfilled. The Romans were followed by the Byzantines, the Arabs, the Crusaders, the Mamlukes, the Turks, the British, and the Jordanians. Finally, after 1,897 years, the city of Jerusalem returned to Jewish hands on June 7, 1967, during the Six-Day War.

End-Time Jerusalem

Four hundred years before Christ, the prophet Zechariah foretold that in the end times Jerusalem would be reoccupied by the Jews (Zechariah 12:6). He also prophesied that the city would become the focal point of world politics:

> I am going to make Jerusalem a cup that causes reeling to all the peoples around.... I will make Jerusalem a heavy stone for all the peoples; all who lift it will be severely injured. And all the nations of the earth will be gathered against it (Zechariah 12:2-3).

This prophecy began to be fulfilled overnight in 1973 when the Arabs pulled their oil boycott. The Western nations went begging to the Arabs for oil. The Arabs responded by quadrupling the price and demanding that the West line up with them in their obsession to destroy Israel and retake Jerusalem. Jerusalem has been the focus of world politics since that time.

Zechariah also prophesied that the Lord would return to this earth at the Mount of Olives during a time when Jerusalem would be under siege and about to fall (Zechariah 14:1-9). In fact, he says that half of the city will have already fallen to the Antichrist and his forces (Zechariah 14:2).

Just as the city is about to be wiped out, "the LORD will go forth and fight against those nations, as when He fights on a day of battle" (Zechariah 14:3). He will destroy the enemy forces (Zechariah 14:12-15), and on that day He "will be king over all the earth" (Zechariah 14:9).

Millennial Jerusalem

Many of the Old Testament prophets predicted that when the Lord Jesus returns He will establish His throne in Jerusalem and will begin a glorious reign over all the nations. Here is the way Isaiah 21:1-3 puts it:

> Now it will come about that
> In the last days,
> The mountain of the house of the LORD
> Will be established as the chief of the moun-
>   tains,
> And will be raised above the hills;
> And all the nations will stream to it.
> And many peoples will come and say,
> "Come, let us go up to the mountain of the
>   LORD,
> To the house of the God of Jacob;
> That He may teach us concerning His ways,
> And that we may walk in His paths,"
> For the law will go forth from Zion,
> And the word of the LORD from Jerusalem.

At that time Jerusalem will be the political, economic, and religious center of the world. The city will be enlarged and beautified, and the most magnificent Temple in all of history will be built under the personal supervision of the Messiah, who will be reigning as king of the world (Ezekiel 40-48).

When this is accomplished, Jerusalem will at long last be established in peace, and the city will be called "the City of Truth" (Zechariah 8:3).

Jerusalem will also become the greatest wonder on the face of the earth. Two things will help bring this about. First, the great earthquake which will occur at the return of the Lord will raise every valley, lower every mountain, and move every island (Revelation 6:12-14). That same quake will lift up Jerusalem like a shining jewel, and the city will become the highest point on the face of the earth (Zechariah 14:10-11 and Micah 4:1).

Even more spectacular, the Shekinah glory of God will return to hover over the city like a canopy, providing shade from the sun and refuge from rain (Isaiah 4:5-6). What a spectacular sight that will be!

Zechariah says that the nations of the world will send delegations to Jerusalem each year for the celebration of the Feast of Tabernacles, and any nation that refuses to do this will experience drought (Zechariah 14:16-17).

Isaiah says that at that time the city will be "a crown of beauty in the hand of the LORD and a royal diadem in the hand of your God" (Isaiah 62:3).

Eternal Jerusalem

Finally, the prophets tell us that the millennial Jerusalem will be replaced by a New Jerusalem which Jesus is preparing in Heaven right now (John 14:1-4). This city will serve as the eternal abode of His saints.

At the end of the Millennium, after the earth has been renovated by fire, the New Jerusalem will be lowered down to the New Earth, and the Redeemed will live in their new bodies in this incredible city in the presence of Almighty God.

Yes, the Bible says that God will come down from Heaven to live forever with His children on the New Earth (Revelation 21:1–22:5). Since Heaven is located wherever God resides, this means that Heaven will come to earth.

And because the Redeemed will be blessed forever with the presence of God, the name of Jerusalem will be changed to "Yahweh-Shammah," which means "The LORD is there" (Ezekiel 48:35).

The very thought is enough to prompt me to cry out, "Maranatha!" (1 Corinthians 16:22).

Your Jerusalem?

What about you? Can you join with me in crying out, "Maranatha!"? That is an Aramaic expression which means, "Our Lord come!"

Are you a candidate for citizenship in the New Jerusalem? The Lord will be there. Will you?

I have a room reserved for me in the New Jerusalem. I know that with certainty because I have placed my faith in Jesus as my Lord and Savior, and by doing so I have become an heir of all the heavenly promises (Revelation 21:7).

What about you? Do you have a room reservation?

13

The Wrath of God

Myth or Reality?

A popular radio talk show host on an Oklahoma City secular station recently interviewed me live on the air via telephone. He had seen an article I had written about the financial accountability of Christian ministries, and he had liked it.

He began the interview by graciously giving me the opportunity to talk nonstop for about ten minutes about the way God had transformed my life and called me into the ministry. We then moved on to a discussion of the scandals that had recently rocked the Christian community nationwide.

The Unmentionable Word

Everything went well until the host asked me to summarize the fundamental message of my ministry. I responded by saying that God had called me to proclaim "the soon return of Jesus in wrath."

Before I could proceed with my explanation, the announcer cut me short. "What do you mean, 'wrath'?" he asked.

"I mean that Jesus is going to return very soon to pour out the wrath of God upon those who have rejected God's love and grace and mercy."

"Your God is a monster God!" he snapped. He then added, "I happen to be a Christian, and I can tell you that my God wouldn't hurt a flea!"

That was the end of the interview. He hung up on me. I was not given an opportunity to respond to his blasphemy.

Satan's Grand Deception

The radio host's vehement response to the wrath of God did not surprise me. It is characteristic of both Christians and non-Christians and I have encountered it many times.

Satan has sold the world a bill of goods concerning the nature of God. Most people, both Christian and non-Christian, tend to view God as being a sort of cosmic teddy bear.

They see Him as big and warm and soft, full of infinite love and forgiveness. He couldn't hurt a fly, and He certainly wouldn't be so cruel as to condemn or harm any beings created in His own image. On the Day of Judgment, God will simply give everyone a big hug and wink at their sins.

The only problem with this wonderfully comforting image is that it is a lie straight from the pit of Hell.

The True God

Yes, the Bible teaches that God is loving, patient, caring, and forgiving (Psalm 86:15 and John 3:16). As the apostle John put it, "God is love" (1 John 4:8).

Two of my favorite passages in the Bible emphasize the personal loving nature of God. One was penned by the apostle Peter. In 1 Peter 5:6-7 he says that we are to cast all our anxieties upon God "because He cares for you." That is a very comforting thought.

The other passage that I love to read over and over was written by the prophet Jeremiah in Lamentations 3:22-24 (RSVB):

> The steadfast love of the LORD never ceases,
> His mercies never come to an end;
> They are new every morning;
> Great is thy faithfulness.
> "The LORD is my portion," says my soul,
> "Therefore I will hope in him."

But the Bible also clearly teaches that there is another aspect of God's character that is equally important. It is the aspect that Satan wants us to ignore, and he has been very successful in prompting ministers to overlook it. After all, it doesn't produce popular sermons! I'm speaking, of course, of the holiness of God (Leviticus 11:44; Isaiah 6:3; 1 Peter 1:16).

Grace or Wrath?

The Bible teaches that God is perfectly holy. Because of this attribute of His character, He cannot tolerate sin (Numbers 14:18). The Bible says God must deal with sin, and He does so in one of two ways—either grace or wrath.

Every person on the face of this earth is at this moment under either the grace of God or the wrath of God. Jesus Himself made this point in His discourse with Nicodemus.

In the same conversation in which Jesus spoke the glorious words about God's love in John 3:16, He also spoke of God's wrath in a verse that we sometimes like to ignore: "He who believes in the Son has eternal life; but he who does not obey the Son shall not see life, but the wrath of God abides on him" (John 3:36).

The apostle Paul emphasized this point in his preaching and teaching. In Ephesians 5 he warns against immorality, covetousness, and idolatry, and then he adds this observation: "Let no one deceive you with empty words, for because of these things, the wrath of God comes upon the sons of disobedience" (Ephesians 5:6).

We come under God's grace by placing our faith in Jesus and appropriating His atoning sacrifice for our lives (1 John 1:7). There is no salvation apart from Jesus (Acts 4:10-12). Those who have rejected God's free gift of grace in Jesus are under God's wrath (John 3:36), and they have no one to blame but themselves.

The Coming Wrath

God's wrath will fall when Jesus returns (Jude 14-15). The passage in Revelation which pictures the return of Jesus says that He will return in righteousness to judge and wage war (Revelation 19:11).

The first time Jesus came, He came in loving compassion with eyes filled with tears. But when He returns, He will come in vengeance (Revelation 6:12-17), with eyes like a flame of fire (Revelation 19:12). He will come to destroy the enemies of God (Revelation 19:11).

The presidents and kings and prime ministers of the world will get on their knees and cry out for the rocks and mountains to fall upon them, so great will be the terror of the Lord (Revelation 6:15-17). The unrighteous will stumble about like blind men, and their blood will be poured out like dust (Zephaniah 1:17).

The Meaning of Wrath

Does this make God a "monster"? No! On the contrary, it proves His goodness, for how could a good God ignore the evil of sin and allow it to go unpunished? His wrath against evil will demonstrate His righteousness.

The prophet Nahum summed it up best. Writing of the love of God, he said, "The LORD is good, a stronghold in the day of trouble, and He knows those who take refuge in Him" (Nahum 1:7). But a few verses earlier Nahum had also spoken of the holiness of God:

> The LORD is avenging and wrathful.
> The LORD takes vengeance on His adver-
> saries,
> And He reserves wrath for His enemies.
> The LORD is slow to anger and great in
> power,
> And the LORD will by no means leave the
> guilty unpunished (Nahum 1:2-3).

God's wrath is never motivated primarily by a desire to punish. Rather, it is designed to bring people to repentance so that they might be saved. Even in His wrath, God remembers mercy.

God demonstrates His mercy in wrath by never pouring out His wrath without warning. He tried to warn Sodom and Gomorrah through Abraham. He warned Noah's world through the preaching of Noah for 120 years. He sent both Jonah and Nahum to warn the pagan city of Nineveh.

Consider too how He sent prophet after prophet to call the nations of Israel and Judah to repentance:

> The LORD, the God of their fathers, sent
> word to them again and again by His mes-
> sengers, because He had compassion on His
> people and on His dwelling place; but they
> continually mocked the messengers of God, de-
> spised His words and scoffed at His prophets,
> until the wrath of the LORD arose against

His people, until there was no remedy
(2 Chronicles 36:15-16).

God's mercy in wrath is also manifested in the fact
that He always leads up to His final outpouring of wrath
through a series of progressive judgments. These judgments are outlined in detail in Deuteronomy 28:15-68.

This characteristic of God's wrath is demonstrated
in the prophecies concerning the Tribulation. Rather
than simply pouring out His wrath on the rebellious
nations of the world, destroying them in one instant of
overwhelming catastrophe, He subjects the world to a
series of judgments that sequentially increase in scope
and intensity (Revelation 6,8,9,16).

Although most people refuse to repent in response to
these judgments (Revelation 9:20-21), there is "a great
multitude, which no one could count, from every nation
and all tribes and peoples and tongues" who do repent
and respond to Jesus in faith (Revelation 7:9).

These radically different responses to the wrath of
God illustrate the point that is often made by Billy
Graham: "The same sun that melts the butter also
hardens the clay." The wrath of God melts some hearts
in repentance, but it has the effect of hardening the
hearts of many others.

Wrath and the Redeemed

Many Christians respond negatively to Bible prophecy. It's not at all unusual to hear a Christian say
something like this: "I don't want to hear anything
about prophecy because it's too full of gloom and doom."

Well, there is a lot of gloom and doom for those who
refuse to respond to God's gift of love in Jesus. But there
is only good news for the Redeemed.

The Old Testament ends with a passage that presents both the gloom and the joy of end-time prophecy.

Malachi says that when the Lord returns, the day will be "like a furnace; and all the arrogant and every evil-doer will be chaff" (Malachi 4:1). That's the bad news.

But consider the good news: "But for you who fear My name the sun of righteousness will rise with healing in its wings; and you will go forth and skip about like calves from the stall" (Malachi 4:2).

There is no reason for any child of God to fear the wrath of God. Paul wrote that since we have been justified by the blood of Christ, "we shall be saved from the wrath of God through Him" (Romans 5:9). And in a most comforting verse, Paul told the Thessalonians that Jesus will "deliver" the Redeemed "from the wrath to come" (1 Thessalonians 1:10). The reason, Paul explained, is that "God has not destined us for wrath, but for obtaining salvation through our Lord Jesus Christ" (1 Thessalonians 5:9).

A Plea

Are you under grace or wrath? The choice is yours. Jesus is coming soon. When He appears, will He be your Blessed Hope or your Holy Terror? Will you cry for the mountains to fall upon you? Or will you go forth leaping with joy like a calf released from a stall?

God loves you and He wants you to accept His Son as your Savior so that you will come under grace and can participate in an event described by Isaiah:

> The ransomed of the LORD will return,
> And come with joyful shouting to Zion,
> With everlasting joy upon their heads.
> They will find gladness and joy,
> And sorrow and sighing will flee away
> (Isaiah 35:10).

14

Eternal Destiny

What Happens When You Die?

If several years ago you had asked me what happens when you die, I would have given you a pathetic answer.

I would have told you that when you die your soul goes to sleep until the Lord returns. At the return of the Lord, your soul is resurrected and judged, and you are either consigned to Hell or allowed to enter Heaven.

My conception of Heaven was that of a spirit world where the saved spend eternity as disembodied spirits, floating around on clouds, playing harps.

A Mistaken View

Naturally, I couldn't get very excited about all that. I sure didn't like the idea of being unconscious for eons of time. Nor could I develop any enthusiasm for the prospect of being a disembodied spirit with no particular identity or personality. And the idea of playing a harp for all eternity was downright scandalous, for I had been taught that instrumental music in worship was an abomination!

You can imagine, therefore, the sense of shock I felt when I started studying Bible prophecy and discovered that all these ideas of mine about life after death were foreign to God's Word. But my shock quickly gave way to exhilaration when I discovered what the Lord really has in store for me.

The Biblical View

I learned from God's Word that when those of us who are Christians die, our spirits never lose their consciousness (Philippians 1:23). Instead, our fully conscious spirits are immediately ushered into the presence of Jesus by His holy angels (2 Corinthians 5:8).

Our spirits remain in the Lord's presence until He appears for His Church. At that time He brings our spirits with Him, resurrects our bodies, reunites our spirits with our bodies, and then glorifies our bodies, perfecting them and rendering them eternal (1 Thessalonians 4:13-18).

We return with Him to Heaven in our glorified bodies where we are judged for our works to determine our degrees of reward (2 Corinthians 5:10). When this judgment is completed, we participate in a glorious wedding feast to celebrate the union of Jesus and His bride, the Church (Revelation 19:7-9).

Witnesses of Glory

At the conclusion of the feast, we burst from the heavens with Jesus, returning with Him to the earth in glory (Revelation 19:14). We witness His victory at Armageddon, we shout, "Hallelujah!" as He is crowned King of kings and Lord of lords, and we revel in His glory as He begins to reign over all the earth from Mount Zion in Jerusalem (Zechariah 14:1-9; Revelation 19:17-21).

For a thousand years we participate in that reign, assisting Him with the instruction, administration, and enforcement of His perfect laws (Revelation 20:1-6). We see the earth regenerated and nature reconciled (Isaiah 11:6-9). We see holiness abound and the earth flooded with peace, righteousness, and justice (Micah 4:1-7).

At the end of the Millennium we witness the release of Satan to deceive the nations. We see the truly despicable nature of the heart of Man as millions rally to Satan in his attempt to overthrow the throne of Jesus. But we will shout "Hallelujah!" again when we witness God's supernatural destruction of Satan's armies and see Satan himself cast into Hell, where he will be tormented forever (Revelation 20:7-10).

We will next witness the Great White Throne Judgment when the unrighteous are resurrected to stand before God. We will see perfect holiness and justice in action as God pronounces His terrible judgment upon this congregation of the damned who have rejected His gift of love and mercy in Jesus Christ (Revelation 20:11-13).

Jesus will be fully vindicated as every knee shall bow and every tongue confess that He is Lord. Then the unrighteous will receive their just reward as they are cast into Hell (Revelation 20:14-15).

Witnesses of a New Creation

We will then witness the most spectacular fireworks display in all of history.

We will be taken to the New Jerusalem, the eternal mansion prepared by Jesus for His bride, and from there we will watch as God renovates this earth with fire, burning away all the filth and pollution left by Satan's last battle (2 Peter 3:12-13).

Just as the angels rejoiced when God created the universe, we will rejoice as we watch God superheat this

earth and reshape it like a hot ball of wax into the New
Earth, the eternal earth, the paradise where we will live
forever in the presence of God (Revelation 21:1).

What a glorious moment it will be when we are
lowered to the New Earth inside the fabulous New Jerusalem (Revelation 21:2). God will come down from
Heaven to dwell with us (Revelation 21:3). He will proclaim: "Behold, I make all things new" (Revelation 21:5).
We will see God face to face (Revelation 22:4). He will
wipe away all our tears, and death will be no more
(Revelation 21:4). We will be given new names (Revelation 2:17), and we will exist as individual personalities
encased in perfect bodies (Philippians 3:21). And we will
grow eternally in knowledge and love of our infinite
Creator, honoring Him with our talents and gifts.

Now, I can get excited about that!

The Word Versus Tradition

Isn't it amazing how far we can drift away from the
Word of God when we stop reading His Word and start
mouthing the traditions of men?

As I kept making one discovery after another in
God's Prophetic Word that ran contrary to what I had
been taught, I began to wonder about the origin of the
doctrines I had learned. It didn't take me long to discover that the source was Greek philosophy.

The first attempt to mix the concepts of Greek philosophy with the teachings of God's Word came very
early in the history of the Church. The attempt was
called Gnosticism. The Gnostic heresy arose among the
first Gentile converts because they tried to Hellenize
the Scriptures; that is, they tried to make the Scriptures
conform to the basic tenets of Greek philosophy.

The Greeks believed that the material universe,
including the human body, was evil. This negative view
of the creation was diametrically opposed to Hebrew

thought, as revealed in the Bible. To the Hebrew mind, the world was created good (Genesis 1:31). And even though the goodness of the creation was corrupted by the sin of Man (Isaiah 24:5-6), the creation still reflects to some degree the glory of God (Psalm 19:1). Most important, the creation will someday be redeemed by God (Romans 8:18-23).

The Gnostic Heresy

When the first Gentiles were converted to the gospel, their Greek mind-set immediately collided with some of the fundamental teachings of Christianity. For example, they wondered, "How could Jesus have come in the flesh if He was God? God is holy. How can He who is holy be encased in a body which is evil?"

In short, because they viewed the material universe as evil, they could not accept the Bible's teaching that God became incarnate in the flesh. Their response was to develop the Gnostic heresy that Jesus was a spirit being or phantom who never took on the flesh and therefore never experienced physical death.

This heresy is denounced strongly in Scripture. In 1 John 4:1-2 we are told to test those who seek our spiritual fellowship by asking them to confess "that Jesus Christ has come in the flesh."

The Augustinian Corruption

About A.D. 400 a remarkable theologian by the name of Saint Augustine attempted to Hellenize what the Scriptures taught about end-time events and life after death. Augustine was very successful in his attempt. His views were adopted by the Council of Ephesus in A.D. 431 and have remained Catholic dogma to this day.

The influence of Greek philosophy would not allow Augustine to accept at face value what the Bible taught about life after death.

For example, the Bible says the saints will spend eternity in glorified bodies on a New Earth (Revelation 21:1-7). Such a concept was anathema to the Greek mind of Augustine. If the material world is evil, then he reasoned that the material world must cease to exist when the Lord returns. Augustine solved the problem by spiritualizing what the Bible said. He did this by arguing that the "new earth" of Revelation 21 is just symbolic language for Heaven.

Augustine's views are held by most professing Christians today, both Catholic and Protestant. That means that most of Christianity today teaches Greek philosophy rather than the Word of God when it comes to the realm of end-time prophecy and life after death.

The Intermediate State

Some of the greatest confusion about life after death relates to the intermediate state between death and eternity. Some people advocate a concept called "soul sleep." They argue that both the saved and unsaved are unconscious after death until the return of Jesus.

But the Bible makes it crystal clear that our spirit does not lose its consciousness at death. The only thing that "falls asleep" is our body—in a symbolic sense. Paul says in 2 Corinthians 5:8 that he would prefer to be "absent from the body and . . . at home with the Lord." In Philippians 1:21 he observes, "For me to live is Christ, and to die is gain." He then adds in verse 23 that his desire is "to depart and be with Christ." Paul certainly did not expect to be in a coma after he died!

If then our spirits retain their consciousness after death, where do they go? The Bible teaches that prior to the resurrection of Jesus, the spirits of the dead went to a place called Hades ("Sheol" in the Old Testament). The spirits existed there consciously in one of two compartments, either Paradise or Torments. This concept is pictured graphically in Jesus' story of the rich man and Lazarus (Luke 16:19-31).

The Bible indicates that after the death of Jesus on the Cross, He descended into Hades and declared to all the spirits there His triumph over Satan (1 Peter 3:18-19; 4:6). The Bible also indicates that after His resurrection, when He ascended into Heaven, Jesus took Paradise with Him, transferring the spirits of dead saints from Hades to Heaven (Ephesians 4:8-9 and 2 Corinthians 12:1-4). The spirits of dead saints are thereafter pictured as being in Heaven before the throne of God (see Revelation 6:9 and 7:9).

The spirits of the righteous dead could not go directly to Heaven before the Cross because their sins were not forgiven. Instead, their sins were merely covered by their faith. The forgiveness of their sins had to await the shedding of the blood of Christ (Leviticus 17:11; Romans 5:8-9; Hebrews 9:22).

Events at Death

So, what happens when you die? If you are a child of God, your spirit is immediately ushered into the bosom of Jesus by His holy angels. Your spirit remains in Heaven, in the presence of God, until the time of the Rapture. When Jesus comes for His Church, He brings your spirit with Him, resurrects and glorifies your body, making it eternal in nature (1 Corinthians 15 and 1 Thessalonians 4). You reign with Christ for a thousand years and then live eternally with Him on the New Earth (Revelation 20-22).

If you are not a child of God, then your spirit goes to Hades at your death. This is a place of torments where your spirit is held until the resurrection of the unrighteous, which takes place at the end of the millennial reign of Jesus. At that resurrection you are taken before the Great White Throne of God where you are judged by your works and then condemned to the "second death," which is the "lake of fire" or Hell (Revelation 20:11-15).

Preparing for Eternity

One thing is certain: Every knee shall bow and every tongue shall confess that Jesus is Lord (Isaiah 45:23; Romans 14:11)! Your eternal destiny will be determined by *when* you make this confession.

If it is made before you die, then you will spend eternity with God. If not, then you will make the confession at the Great White Throne Judgment before you are cast into Hell. To spend eternity with God, your confession of Jesus as Lord must be made *now*.

> If you confess with your mouth Jesus as Lord, and believe in your heart that God raised Him from the dead, you shall be saved (Romans 10:9).

15

Resurrections and Judgments

How Many and When?

My boyhood church always taught that there would be one resurrection and one judgment. Everyone who had ever lived would be resurrected at one time, and all of us—the just and the unjust—would be judged at the same time. The sheep would be separated from the goats at the Great White Throne Judgment pictured in Revelation 20:11-15.

But this concept is all wrong. The Bible reveals that there will be more than one resurrection and more than one judgment.

Multiple Resurrections

Jesus clearly taught that there would be more than one resurrection. In John 5:29 He refers to a "resurrection of life" and a "resurrection of judgment." The apostle Paul confirmed this concept in his defense before

Felix when he stated that he believed the teaching of the prophets "that there shall certainly be a resurrection of both the righteous and the wicked" (Acts 24:15).

Of course, it could be argued that the two resurrections referred to in these Scriptures will occur at the same time. Thus, because they will happen simultaneously, there is, in effect, only one resurrection. However, the Scriptures establish the fact that the resurrection of the righteous will occur in stages.

In other words, the Bible does not teach one resurrection or even two resurrections in *number*. Rather, it teaches that there will be two resurrections in *type* which will be conducted in stages, resulting in several resurrections—at least four, to be specific.

The Resurrection of the Just

That the resurrection of the righteous will occur in stages is clearly taught in 1 Corinthians 15:20-24. In fact, the first stage of the resurrection of the righteous has already happened, for verse 20 says that "Christ has been raised from the dead, the first fruits of those who are asleep."

Verses 22 and 23 go on to explain that all who have died in Christ shall be made alive, "but each in his own order: Christ, the first fruits, after that those who are Christ's at His coming."

The imagery of the harvest that is used in these verses is a key to understanding the first resurrection— the resurrection of the righteous.

The Harvest Imagery

In Bible times the harvest was conducted in three stages. It began with the gathering of the firstfruits, which were offered as a sacrifice of thanksgiving to God.

It proceeded with the general harvest. But not all was taken in this harvest. Some of the crop was left in the field to be gathered by the poor and the needy. This was called the gleanings (Leviticus 19:9-10).

Using this imagery, the Bible presents a resurrection of Jesus as the "firstfruits" of the resurrection of the righteous. The gathering of the Church Age saints, living and dead, at the appearing of the Lord (the Rapture) is thus the general harvest stage of the resurrection of the righteous (John 14:1-3 and 1 Thessalonians 4:13-18).

But there is a third and final stage to this resurrection of the righteous. It is the gleanings, and it occurs at the end of the Tribulation when the Lord's Second Coming takes place. At that time two final groups of the righteous will be resurrected: 1) the Tribulation martyrs (Revelation 20:4) and 2) the Old Testament saints (Daniel 12:2).

Some people are startled by the thought that the Old Testament saints will not be resurrected until the end of the Tribulation. But keep in mind that the Rapture is a promise to the Church, and the Church only. Also, the book of Daniel makes it clear that the Old Testament saints will be resurrected at the end of the "time of distress" (Daniel 12:1-2).

So the first resurrection, the resurrection of the righteous, occurs in three stages, beginning with Christ, continuing with the Church at the Rapture, and culminating with the Tribulation martyrs and the Old Testament saints at the return of Jesus.

The Resurrection of the Unjust

The second type of resurrection, "a resurrection of... the wicked" (Acts 24:15), will take place all at one time at the end of the Millennial Reign of Jesus. This is at the time of the Great White Throne Judgment, the judgment of the damned (Revelation 20:11-15).

Every person who ever failed to relate to God in faith will be resurrected at this time, regardless of when he or she may have lived and died—whether before or after the Cross. This resurrection will also include the unjust who died during the Tribulation and the Millennium.

There will be no need for an additional resurrection of the righteous at the end of the Millennium, because all those born during that time who accept Jesus as their Savior will live to the end of the Lord's reign (Isaiah 65:19-20). "'As the lifetime of a tree, so shall be the days of My people,'... says the LORD" (Isaiah 65:22,25). In other words, life spans during the Millennium will be returned to what they were at the beginning of time, before the Flood.

The Certainty of Judgment

Resurrection will be followed by judgment. Solomon wrote, "Fear God and keep His commandments.... Because God will bring every act to judgment, everything which is hidden, whether it is good or evil" (Ecclesiastes 12:13-14).

The apostle Paul emphasized the certainty of judgment. In Romans 2:16 he wrote, "God will judge the secrets of men through Christ Jesus." And in Romans 14:10,12 he stated, "We shall all stand before the judgment seat of God.... So then each one of us shall give account of himself to God." The writer to the Hebrews summed it up succinctly: "It is appointed for men to die once and after this comes judgment" (Hebrews 9:27).

The Completed Judgment

But not all people are going to be judged at the same time. Just as there are going to be several resurrections, there are also going to be several judgments.

One judgment has already taken place. It is the judgment of believers for their sins.

This comes as a surprise to most Christians. Some find it hard to believe. I'll never forget when I realized this fact from my study of Scripture. I became filled with so much joy that I felt like jumping pews all day!

Let me put it to you in another way. If you are truly born again, you will never stand before the Lord and be judged of your sins. That's because the judgment for your sins took place at the Cross.

You see, all your sins, and mine, were placed upon Jesus as He hung upon the Cross, and the wrath we deserve was poured out upon Him (2 Corinthians 5:21). He became our substitute. He took our judgment for sin (Romans 8:3 and Galatians 3:13).

If you have appropriated the blood of Jesus to your life by accepting Him as your Lord and Savior, then your sins have been forgiven. They have also been forgotten in the sense that God will never remember them against you again (Isaiah 43:25 and Hebrews 8:12).

Think of it—forgiven and forgotten! That is grace!

The Judgment of the Just

If the Redeemed will never be judged of their sins, then what will they be judged of, and when will the judgment take place?

The Bible teaches that the Redeemed will be judged of their works, not to determine their eternal destiny, but to determine their degrees of reward.

Christians do not work to be saved; they work *because* they are saved. In fact, the Bible says they are saved to do good works (Ephesians 2:10 and Titus 2:14). Such good works, if properly done, will be done in the power of the Holy Spirit (1 Peter 4:11) and for the glory of God (1 Corinthians 10:31).

The Significance of Spiritual Gifts

Paul says in 1 Corinthians 12 that every person who is born again receives at least one supernatural spiritual gift from the Holy Spirit. A person may receive more than one gift. If you are a good steward of the gifts you receive, you may receive additional gifts as you develop spiritually (Luke 19:26).

God expects us to use our spiritual gifts to advance His kingdom. This is what the judgment of works will be all about. Each of us who are redeemed will stand before the Lord Jesus and give an accounting of how we used our gifts to advance the kingdom of God on earth.

We will be judged as to the *quantity* of our works (Luke 19:11-27; Romans 2:6-7). We will be judged as to the *quality* of our works (1 Corinthians 3:10-14). Finally, we will be judged as to the *motivation* of our works (1 Corinthians 4:5).

I can imagine some famous evangelist being brought before the Lord for judgment.

"How did you use your spiritual gifts to advance my kingdom?" asks the Lord.

"I used my gifts as a teacher and evangelist to preach the gospel to millions," replies the preacher.

"Yes," says the Lord, "you certainly did that. But I know your heart, and thus I know your motivation. You preached not because you loved Me but because you wanted to become famous. You wanted to have your picture published on the cover of *Time* magazine. You accomplished that in February of 1953. Here's your picture. That's all the reward I have for you!"

And then I can imagine the Lord calling up a little old lady that no one has ever heard of.

"Dear, on the day you accepted Me as your Lord and Savior, I gave you one gift—the gift of mercy. Every time someone was ill, you were the first to offer comfort and encouragement. You were the one who organized the prayer chain. Every time someone went to the hospital, you were the first to visit him or her. Every time someone died, you were the one who organized the meals. And you did all of these things simply because you loved Me."

The Lord will give her a crown full of so many jewels that she will have a neckache for eternity!

Seriously, there will be degrees of reward. They will be manifested in the crowns we receive (2 Timothy 4:7-8), the robes we wear (Revelation 19:8), and the degrees of ruling authority which we exercise with the Lord (Luke 19:11-27).

The Timing of the Judgments

When and where will the judgment of the Redeemed take place? The Bible indicates the judgment of believers who have lived and died during the Church Age will occur in Heaven before the judgment seat of Jesus, immediately following the Rapture of the Church (2 Corinthians 5:10 and Revelation 19:6-9).

Those who are saved and martyred during the Tribulation will be judged at the end of that period when they are resurrected at the Second Coming of Christ (Revelation 20:4). The Tribulation saints who live to the end of that terrible period are another group that will be judged at the Second Coming of Jesus in the sheep and goat judgment portrayed in Matthew 25:31-46. The Old Testament saints will also be judged at the time of the Second Coming (Ezekiel 20:34-38).

All the unrighteous who have ever lived will be resurrected and judged at the end of the Millennial Reign of Jesus.

The Judgment of the Unjust

The terrible judgment of the unrighteous is pictured in Revelation 20:11-15. It is called the Great White Throne Judgment.

We are told that the wicked also will be judged by their works. But their judgment will be radically different from the judgment of the Redeemed. Whereas the Redeemed are judged by their works to determine *degrees of reward*, the lost are judged by their works to determine their *eternal destiny*.

And since no one can be justified before God by works (Isaiah 64:6 and Ephesians 2:8-10), all unbelievers will be condemned to Hell. That's why I call this judgment "the judgment of the damned."

The unjust are also judged for another reason: There are going to be degrees of punishment (Luke 12:35-48; 20:45-47).

A popular myth in Christendom says, "All sin is equal in the eyes of God." That is not true. The only way in which all sin is equal is that *any* sin, whether a white lie or murder, condemns us before God and necessitates a Savior.

But all sin is not equal in the eyes of God. For example, Proverbs 6:16-19 lists seven sins that the Lord particularly hates, including "hands that shed innocent blood." And the Bible makes it very clear that idolatry is a sin that is especially heinous in the eyes of God (Exodus 20:3-5).

Because God considers some sins worse than others, there will be degrees of punishment (Revelation 22:12), and these degrees will be specified at the Great White Throne Judgment.

A Call to Repentance

Where do you stand with respect to the inevitable judgment which you will face before the Lord?

If you are a Christian, do you know what spiritual gifts you have been given? Are you using them to advance the Lord's kingdom? Is your motivation a love of the Lord?

If you have never confessed Jesus as your Lord and Savior, do you really want to participate in the judgment of the damned? Do you realize that the Bible says every knee shall bow and every tongue confess that

Jesus is Lord? That means Hitler and every vile person like him who has ever lived will one day make the confession of Jesus' lordship. You will, too.

I urge you to make that confession *now* so that you can participate in the resurrection and judgment of the righteous. As you consider your decision, weigh carefully the following words from the book of Hebrews:

> Christ also, having been offered once to bear the sins of many, shall appear a second time for salvation without reference to sin, to those who eagerly await Him (Hebrews 9:28).

This verse promises that for those who are ready for Him, Jesus will come "without reference to sin." That is a wonderful promise.

16

The Meaning of Heaven

Ethereal or Tangible?

For many years I had little desire to go to Heaven. My only interest in Heaven was prompted by a desire to avoid Hell.

I just couldn't get excited about being a disembodied spirit residing in an ethereal world, floating around on a cloud playing a harp.

My interest in Heaven developed slowly over a long period of time. It became a passion, not as a result of my study of prophecy, but because of my growing relationship with the Lord.

The more I came to know Him, the more I desired to be with Him.

The New Earth

The reason my study of prophecy did not play the key role in developing my interest in Heaven is because the

Bible is strangely silent about the subject. The Bible tells us in great detail what the Millennium will be like, but it gives us almost no detailed information about the eternal state.

What it does tell us often comes as a great surprise to most Christians because the Scriptures about Heaven have been so terribly spiritualized. For example, the Bible plainly says the Redeemed will spend eternity on a New Earth.

Isaiah was the first to speak of this truth when he spoke of "the new heavens and the new earth" which will endure forever before the Lord (Isaiah 66:22). This truth is repeated in the book of Revelation, where the apostle John says he was shown a New Earth, "for the first heaven and the first earth passed away" (Revelation 21:1).

John goes on to describe the New Jerusalem descending to the New Earth, "coming down out of heaven from God" (Revelation 21:2). And then he states that God Himself will come to live on the New Earth:

> Behold, the tabernacle of God is among
> men, and He shall dwell among them, and
> they shall be His people, and God Himself
> shall be among them (Revelation 21:3).

This truth had already been revealed to the Old Testament prophets. While being taken on a prophetic tour of the Millennial Temple, Ezekiel was told by his guide (the Lord Jesus in a preincarnate appearance): "Son of man, this is the place of My throne and the place of the soles of My feet, where I will dwell among the sons of Israel forever" (Ezekiel 43:7).

The Redeemed are going to dwell forever in new bodies on a New Earth in a New Jerusalem in the presence of Almighty God and His Son, Jesus. Heaven will come to earth!

The New Jerusalem

The most detailed information which the Scriptures give about Heaven pertains to our eternal abode—the New Jerusalem. Twenty verses in chapter 21 of Revelation are devoted to a description of it.

The information contained in Revelation 21 is not the first reference in the Bible to the New Jerusalem. It is mentioned in Hebrews 11:10 as a city "whose architect and builder is God." Jesus made a reference to it in John 14:1-4. He called it His "Father's house," and He said He would prepare a place in it for His Church.

Jesus is currently expanding, embellishing, and beautifying this house which God the Father designed and built. Jesus is preparing it for His bride, just as in Old Testament times a bridegroom would add a room onto his father's house to accommodate himself and his bride.

The city is described in Revelation as beautifully decorated, like "a bride adorned for her husband" (Revelation 21:2). Later, John actually refers to the city as the bride of the Lamb (Revelation 21:9), because the city contains the bride of Christ, His Church.

I believe this implies that at the end of the Millennium all the Redeemed will be taken off the earth and placed in the New Jerusalem, which will most likely be suspended in the heavens. From that vantage point we will watch as God burns up this earth and reshapes it like a hot ball of wax into a New Earth, a perfected earth like the one which God created in the beginning. Then we will be lowered down to the New Earth inside the New Jerusalem.

The city will be spectacular in both size and appearance. It will be in the form of a cube that is 1,500 miles in every direction! And it will reflect "the glory of God" (Revelation 21:11,23).

The Size of the City

The incredible size means the city would stretch from Canada to the Gulf of Mexico and from the Atlantic coast of America to Colorado. It would also extend 1,500 miles into the atmosphere.

This tremendous extension of the city vertically into the air is a clue that the New Earth may be considerably larger than the current earth. Otherwise the city would not be proportional to its surroundings.

Would such a city be able to adequately accommodate all the Redeemed? That's a good question. The best answer I have ever seen was provided by Henry Morris in his book *The Revelation Record*.

Dr. Morris postulates the total number of Redeemed might be as many as 20 billion. He further guesses that approximately 75 percent of the New Jerusalem might be devoted to streets, parks, and public buildings. Can 20 billion people be squeezed into only 25 percent of the space of this city?

The answer is yes! In fact, it can be done easily. Each person would have a cubical block with about 75 acres of surface on each face. We are talking about an immense city!

This assumes, of course, that our new glorified bodies will be immune to the current law of gravity, as are the bodies of angels. This is a safe assumption, for 1 John 3:2 says that our glorified bodies will be like the body of Jesus after His resurrection, and His body was not subject to gravity, as evidenced by His ascension into Heaven.

This is the reason the city will be so tall. We will be able to utilize and enjoy all levels of it. There will be vertical streets as well as horizontal ones.

The Beauty of the City

And what streets they will be! The Bible says they will be "pure gold, like transparent glass" (Revelation

21:21). In fact, the whole city will be made of pure gold with the appearance of clear glass (Revelation 21:18).

The city will sit on a foundation made of 12 layers of precious stones (Revelation 21:19-20). Each layer will feature the name of one of the 12 apostles (Revelation 21:14). The city will be surrounded by a jasper wall over 200 feet high (Revelation 21:17). There will be 12 gates, three on each side, and each one will be named for one of the tribes of Israel (Revelation 21:12).

And yes, the gates will be "pearly gates," each one consisting of one huge pearl (Revelation 21:21).

Best of all, God the Father and Jesus will both reside in the city with us (Revelation 21:22). The Shekinah glory of God will illuminate the city constantly, and thus there will be no night nor will there ever be any need for any type of artificial light or the light of the sun (Revelation 22:5).

The throne of God and His Son will be in the city, and "a river of the water of life, clear as crystal" will flow down the middle of the city's main street with the tree of life growing on both sides of the river, yielding 12 kinds of fruit—a different fruit each month (Revelation 22:1-2).

That's it. God's Word only gives us a glimpse of Heaven. But what a tantalizing glimpse it is! It's a glimpse of perfect peace and joy and beauty.

The Activities of Heaven

What will we do for eternity? Again, the Word is strangely silent. All it says is that we "shall serve Him" (Revelation 22:3).

I have fantasized a lot about our heavenly activities. I can imagine us spending a great deal of our time in worship, singing the psalms of King David, with him directing us. I think it is likely that our talents will be magnified, and we will be able to sing or paint or write with a majesty and scope we never imagined possible— and all to the glory of God!

Surely we will spend considerable time in the study of God's Word. Think of studying the Gospel of John with the apostle John as the teacher! I thrill to the thought of Jesus teaching the Old Testament, even as He did to His disciples following His resurrection (Luke 24:44-45). The Word of God is infinite in its depth, and I believe we will continue learning from it forever.

As we study the Word, I believe we will grow in spiritual maturity in the likeness of Jesus. And since God is infinite, no matter how much we grow in His likeness, there will just be that much more growing ahead of us. In this regard, I suspect that our spiritual growth will pick up where it left off in this life.

Sometimes I really get far-out in my thinking about Heaven. Might the Lord give us the opportunity to see "instant video replays" of great events in Bible history? I hope so. I would like to see the dividing of the Red Sea, the destruction of Jericho, and the resurrection of Lazarus.

And what about tours of the universe? Surely we will be able to travel through space in our glorified bodies and see the miracles of God's creation up close. Imagine visiting all the planets in our galaxy as well as touring thousands of other galaxies!

But what does Revelation 22:3 mean when it says we will serve God as His "bond-servants"? I'm not sure. I suppose it means we will be given productive work to do. What that work will be I can't say for sure. But there is a hint in Revelation 22:5, where it says we will reign with the Lord "forever and ever."

To reign necessarily implies that we must reign over someone. Who will that be? Again, there is an intriguing clue. Revelation 21:24-27 refers to "nations" that will live on the New Earth outside the New Jerusalem. Revelation 22:2 indicates that the people composing these nations will be in fleshly bodies, for it says that the leaves of the tree of life will be used for "the healing of the nations."

Who are these "nations"? This is one of the greatest mysteries of Bible prophecy. There are as many different guesses as there are commentaries on the book of Revelation.

Could they be the Redeemed who accept Jesus during the Millennium? Nothing is said about the ultimate destiny of those who are saved during the Millennium. No promises are made to them of glorified bodies.

I don't know the answer. It is one of those areas where we look into a dimly lit mirror and will not understand fully until we stand "face to face" with the Lord (1 Corinthians 13:12).

Heavenly Fellowship

This brings me to the greatest blessing of Heaven. Revelation 22:4 says we shall see the face of God!

The Word says in Exodus 33:20 that no man has ever seen the face of God. But we will be given that privilege when we fellowship with Him in Heaven.

And that is really what Heaven is all about. We will experience an intimacy with the Lord that transcends anything possible in this life. We were created for fellowship with God (John 4:23), and that purpose will reach its zenith in the eternal state as we live in God's presence.

That is why Paul wrote, "To live is Christ, and to die is gain" (Philippians 1:21). He went on to explain that to continue living in the flesh meant the opportunity for fruitful labor in the Lord's kingdom. But he still had a desire to depart this life, for that departure would open the door for sweet, intimate, personal fellowship with the Lord (Philippians 1:22-23).

What about you? Are you clinging to this world, or do you yearn for Heaven?

The more you come to know the Lord, the more you will love Him. And the more you love Him, the more You will desire to be with Him.

That's only natural. We always desire to be with those whom we love.

Longing for Heaven

I love my wife dearly. We have been married for more than 30 years. I have to travel a lot. I call her every night I'm on the road to tell her that I love her. I send her mushy love cards. And when I have to be gone for an extended period, I send her gifts like bouquets of flowers.

I love to talk with my wife by phone. I love to send her love notes. I love to surprise her with gifts. But none of these are substitutes for being with her! When you love someone you want to be with him or her.

In like manner, I love to fellowship with the Lord in worship, in Bible study, and in prayer. But these spiritual activities are no substitute for actually being with the Lord.

Because I love Him, I want to be with Him. Personal, intimate fellowship with the Lord—that is the essence of Heaven. May it become a reality very soon!

17

The Nature of Hell

Eternal Punishment or Eternal Torment?

The Bible presents Hell, like Heaven, as a real place. The Bible says that God created this terrible place to serve as the ultimate destiny of the Devil and his angels (Matthew 25:41). The Bible also teaches that Hell will be the destiny of all people who reject the grace and mercy God has provided through Jesus and who choose instead to reject God by following Satan (Matthew 25:46).

Hell is described in the Scriptures as a place of darkness and sadness (Matthew 22:13), a place of fire (Matthew 5:22), a place of torment (Revelation 14:10), a place of destruction (Matthew 7:13), and a place of disgrace and everlasting contempt (Daniel 12:2).

Its Distinction from Hades

Hell is not Hades. A careful study of the Scriptures will reveal that Hades in the New Testament is the same place as Sheol in the Old Testament (Psalm 49:15).

Let's review a few points that I made earlier in the chapter on death. Before the Cross, Hades (or Sheol) was the holding place for the spirits of the dead who awaited their resurrection, judgment, and ultimate consignment to Heaven or Hell. According to Jesus' story of the rich man and Lazarus (Luke 16:19-31), Hades was composed of two compartments—Paradise and Torments. At death, the spirits of the righteous (those who had put their faith in God) went to a compartment in Hades called Paradise. The unrighteous went to a compartment called Torments. The two compartments were separated by a wide gulf that could not be crossed.

The Bible indicates that the nature of Hades was radically changed at the time of the Cross. After His death on the Cross, Jesus descended into Hades and declared to all the spirits there His triumph over Satan through the shedding of His blood for the sins of Mankind (1 Peter 3:18-9; 4:6).

The Bible also indicates that after His resurrection, when He ascended to Heaven, Jesus took Paradise with Him, transferring the spirits of the righteous dead from Hades to Heaven (Ephesians 4:8-9 and 2 Corinthians 12:1-4). The spirits of the righteous dead are thereafter pictured as being in Heaven before the throne of God (Revelation 6:9 and 7:9).

Thus, since the time of the Cross, the spirits of dead saints no longer go to Hades. Instead, they are taken directly to Heaven. The spirits of Old Testament saints could not go directly to Heaven because their sins had not been forgiven. Their sins had only been covered, so to speak, by their faith. Their sins could not be forgiven until Jesus shed His blood for them on the Cross.

The souls of the unrighteous dead will remain in Hades until the end of the Millennial Reign of Jesus. At that time they will be resurrected and judged at the

Great White Throne Judgment portrayed in Revelation 20:11-15. They will be judged by their works, and since no person can be justified before God by works (Ephesians 2:8-10), all the unrighteous will be cast into Hell, which the passage in Revelation refers to as "the lake of fire" (Revelation 20:14).

The Duration of Hell

How long will the unrighteous be tormented in Hell? The traditional view holds that Hell is a place of eternal, conscious torment. According to this view, a person who winds up in Hell is doomed to a never-ending existence of excruciating pain and suffering. Hell is a place of no escape and no hope.

Another point of view—the one I hold—takes the position that immortality is conditional, depending upon one's acceptance of Christ. I believe the Bible teaches the unrighteous will be resurrected, judged, punished in Hell for a period of time proportional to their sins, and then suffer destruction (the death of body and soul).

In a moment we will take a brief look at both views, but before we do, I would like to remind us all of a sobering truth: Hell is a reality, and it is a dreadful destiny. Hell exists because God cannot be mocked (Galatians 6:7). He is going to deal with sin, and He deals with sin in one of two ways—either grace or wrath. John 3:36 says, "He who believes in the Son has eternal life; but he who does not obey the Son shall not see life, but the wrath of God abides on him."

Whatever we conclude from the Scriptures about the duration of Hell, we must remember that Hell is to be avoided at all costs. Whether the wicked suffer there eternally or are destroyed after enduring God's terrible punishment, Hell is an unimaginably terrifying place.

We must also remember that our beliefs about the duration of Hell are not on the plane of cardinal doctrine. Sincere, godly Christians may study the same Scripture passages about Hell and end up with differing conclusions about the issue of its duration. Our varied viewpoints, arrived at through earnest and godly study, should not be allowed to cause division or rancor in the body of Christ.

The Traditional Viewpoint

Few traditionalists are happy about the doctrine of the eternal torment of the wicked, but they accept it anyway because they believe it to be biblical. In this they are to be commended.

Most point to Scriptures such as Matthew 25:46 for support: "And these [the wicked] will go away into eternal punishment, but the righteous into eternal life." Since the word "eternal" is used of both the wicked and the righteous, they conclude that the punishment must be eternal in the same way that the life is.

Many traditionalists also cite Revelation 20:10—a verse specifically about the Devil, the Antichrist, and the False Prophet—to prove that a God of love can indeed sentence at least some of His creatures to eternal torment: "And the devil who deceived them was thrown into the lake of fire and brimstone, where the beast and the false prophet are also; and they will be tormented day and night forever and ever." If it is possible for God to treat one set of His creatures in this way, they reason, why should it be impossible for Him to do the same thing with another set?

Still another Revelation passage also figures in the traditionalist argument. Revelation 14:9-11 reads:

> And another angel, a third one, followed
> them, saying with a loud voice, "If anyone

worships the beast and his image, and
receives a mark on his forehead or upon his
hand, he also will drink of the wine of the
wrath of God, which is mixed in full strength
in the cup of His anger; and he will be tormented with fire and brimstone in the
presence of the holy angels and in the presence of the Lamb. And the smoke of their
torment goes up forever and ever; and they
have no rest day and night, those who worship the beast and his image, and whoever
receives the mark of his name."

Traditionalists notice that not only are these unbelievers tossed into the lake of fire where "the smoke of
their torment goes up forever and ever," but they have
no rest "day or night." This is in stark contrast to the
saved, who will enjoy rest eternally (Revelation 14:13).
To traditionalists, both the "rest" of believers and the
"unrest" of unbelievers seem to imply a conscious state.

Other Traditionalist Arguments

In other parts of the Bible, several passages which
talk about Hell use the word "destroy" or "destruction"
to describe what happens to the unrighteous. Traditionalists claim that the picture in these passages is not
of obliteration but of a ruin of human life out of God's
presence forever. In this way they are able to conceive of
a "destruction" which lasts forever.

A more philosophical traditionalist argument concerns Mankind's creation in the image of God. Some
traditionalists believe that the torments of Hell must be
eternal, since humankind was made in the image of God
and that image cannot be "uncreated." Thus they
believe that immortality was bestowed on Mankind
when God created male and female in His image.

Last, many traditionalists believe that Hell must be eternal because of the nature of sin itself. All sin is an offense against God, goes this argument, and since God is infinite, all sin is infinitely odious. Jonathan Edwards, the great Puritan theologian, took this line of argument in his book *The Justice of God in the Damnation of Sinners.*

As you can see, these arguments seem both biblical and substantial. And yet they are not without significant problems. Allow me to explain why I believe the conditionalist approach is a better solution to the difficulty.

The Conditionalist Viewpoint

The doctrine of the duration of Hell has been so strongly held throughout the history of Christianity that few have dared to challenge it. Adding to the reluctance has been the fact that most modern challenges have come from the cults. Thus, a person who dares to question the traditional viewpoint runs the risk of being labeled a cultist.

A classic characteristic of modern-day "Christian" cults is their denial of the reality of Hell. Some argue that everyone will be saved. Most take the position that the unrighteous are annihilated at physical death.

The views of the cults regarding Hell have always been repulsive to me because they deny the clear teaching of Scripture that the unrighteous will be sent to a place of suffering called Hell. Yet, I have never been able to fully embrace the traditional viewpoint of conscious, eternal punishment.

Traditionalist Difficulties

My first difficulty with the traditional view is that it seems to impugn the character of God. I kept asking myself, "How could a God of grace, mercy, and love torment the vast majority of humanity eternally?" It did not seem to me to be either loving or just. I realize He is a God of righteousness, holiness, and justice, but is eternal suffering *justice?* The concept of eternal torment seems to convert the true God of justice into a cosmic sadist.

Second, the concept of eternal torment seems to run contrary to biblical examples. God destroyed Sodom and Gomorrah with fire—suddenly and quickly. He destroyed Noah's evil world with water—suddenly and quickly. He ordered the Canaanites to be killed swiftly. In the Law of Moses there was no provision for incarceration or torture. Punishments for violation of the Law consisted either of restitution or death. Even sacrificial animals were spared suffering through precise prescriptions for their killing that guaranteed a death that would be as quick and painless as possible.

As a student of God's Prophetic Word, I found a third problem with the traditional view. It seems to contradict a descriptive phrase that is used in prophecy to describe Hell. That term is "the second death." It is a term peculiar to the book of Revelation (Revelation 2:11; 20:6,14; 21:8). How can Hell be a "second death" if it consists of eternal, conscious torment?

The Problem of Destruction

A fourth reason the traditional view has always troubled me is that it seems to ignore an important biblical teaching about Hell—namely, that Hell is a place of *destruction*. Jesus Himself spoke of Hell as a place of "destruction" (Matthew 7:13). Further, in Matthew 10:28 Jesus says, "Do not fear those who kill the body, but are unable to kill the soul; but rather fear Him who is able to destroy both soul and body in hell."

Likewise, in 2 Thessalonians 1:9 Paul says that those who do not obey the gospel "will pay the penalty of eternal destruction." The writer of Hebrews says that the unrighteous will experience a terrifying judgment that will result in their consumption by fire (Hebrews 10:27). Even one of the most comforting verses in the Bible speaks of the destruction of the unrighteous: "For God so loved the world, that He gave His only begotten Son, that whoever believes in Him should not *perish*, but have eternal life" (John 3:16).

The traditionalist argument that the word "destroy" or "destruction" should be interpreted as "irreparable loss" seems a stretch to me. It seems much more likely that "destroy" should be taken to mean exactly that.

The Meaning of Punishment

Fifth, there is a difference between eternal punish-*ment* and eternal punish*ing*. It is one thing to experience a punishment that is eternal in its consequences; it is another thing to experience eternal punishing.

The Bible also speaks of eternal judgment (Hebrews 6:2). Is that a judgment that continues eternally, or is it a judgment with eternal consequences? Likewise, the Bible speaks of eternal redemption (Hebrews 9:12). But this does not mean that Christ will continue the act of redemption eternally. That act took place at the Cross, once and for all. It was an eternal redemption because the result of the redemption had eternal consequences.

Symbolism

Sixth, I noted earlier that traditionalists often cite Revelation 14:9-11 to demonstrate that the suffering of the wicked will be eternal. They most often highlight two phrases. The first refers to those who take the mark of the beast during the Tribulation, who will be "tormented with fire and brimstone in the presence of the holy angels." The second is that "the smoke of their torment goes up forever and ever." Notice that this passage does not speak of eternal torment. Rather, it speaks of "the smoke of their torment" ascending forever.

The Bible is its own best interpreter, and when you look up statements similar to this you will find that they are symbolic for a punishment that has eternal consequences, not a punishment that continues eternally. For example, consider Isaiah 34:10, which speaks of the destruction of Edom. It says the smoke of Edom's destruction will "go up forever."

I have been to Edom (the southern portion of modern-day Jordan in the area around Petra). I have seen its destruction. But there was no smoke ascending to heaven. The reference to eternal smoke is obviously symbolic, indicating that Edom's destruction will give eternal testimony to how God deals with a sinful society.

The same is true of Jude 7 when it says that Sodom and Gomorrah experienced "the punishment of eternal fire." Again, I have been to the area at the southern tip of the Dead Sea where these twin cities existed. The area is one of utter devastation, but there is no smoke going up to heaven. They are not burning eternally. They simply suffered a fiery destruction that had eternal consequences.

Immortality

Last, many traditionalists believe that the soul is immortal. But is it? I believe the Bible denies the immortality of the soul point-blank.

In 1 Timothy 6:15-16 Paul says that God alone possesses immortality. And 1 Corinthians 15:53 teaches that the Redeemed will not become immortal until the time of their resurrection.

In other words, immortality is a gift of God which He gives in His grace to the Redeemed at the time of their resurrection. There is no need to believe in an eternal Hell if the soul is not intrinsically immortal. And it isn't.

Can History Decide the Question?

You should see by now that both the traditional and the conditional positions on Hell can muster good, biblical support for their point of view. Can Church history help us decide which is right?

Unfortunately, it cannot, for both viewpoints can be found in very early writings. The idea of a Hell where the impenitent were eternally tormented can be traced to a time even before Jesus. The intertestamental *Book of Enoch,* as well as the *Fourth Book of the Sibylline Oracles,* both speak of the eternal suffering of the wicked. The great Rabbi Hillel, who lived at about the same time as Jesus, taught that one class of sinner would be punished "to ages of ages"—even though he maintained that most of the damned would be annihilated.

These are all non-Christian sources. But Cyprian, a Christian from the third century, wrote that "the damned will burn forever in hell." If we ask who was responsible for systematizing and popularizing the traditional viewpoint, we find that it was Augustine around the year A.D. 400. But the position certainly was taught before his time.

The conditionalist viewpoint can also be traced back to Bible times. For example, it can be found in the writings of Justin Martyr (A.D. 114-165). In his *Dialogue with Trypho the Jew,* Martyr states that the soul is mortal, that the souls of the unrighteous will suffer only as long as God wills, and that finally their souls will pass out of existence. The concept is also affirmed in the *Didache,* a second-century Christian handbook. That book speaks of "two ways"—the way of life and the way of death. It says the unrighteous will perish.

The Reality of Hell

Which viewpoint is right? I have already cast my vote for the conditionalist understanding. You may decide that the evidence points in the other direction.

But whatever you conclude, based on our study of Scripture, we can agree that Hell is a terrifying, horrendous, ghastly place that should be avoided at all costs. You certainly do not want your friends or your family to go there—there will be no parties in hell!—and you should do all you can to make sure it is not your final home.

The truth is—as I have stressed repeatedly—your eternal destiny is in your hands. You can choose eternal life by receiving Jesus as your Lord and Savior. Or you can choose eternal destruction by refusing to accept God's gift of love and grace. I urge you to choose life by accepting Jesus (Deuteronomy 30:15-19).

3

Prophetic Views

*"The LORD will be king over all the
earth; in that day the LORD will be the
only one, and His name the only one."*
—Zechariah 14:9

18

End-Time Viewpoints

Why So Many Different Concepts?

I almost gave up studying Bible prophecy the very first week I started. I was turned off by the vocabulary.

I kept running across terms like premillennial, amillennial, and postmillennial. It sounded to me like much of prophecy was written in tongues!

Thankfully, the Holy Spirit encouraged me to stick with the task, and before long I began to realize that the terms really were not all that difficult to understand.

Basically, there are four major end-time viewpoints. Or, to put it another way, there are four different interpretations about what the Bible says concerning end-time events.

Historic Premillennialism

The oldest viewpoint is called historic premillennialism. It is termed "historic" for two reasons: to

differentiate it from modern premillennialism and to
indicate that it was the historic position of the early
Church.

It is called "premillennial" because it envisions a
return of Jesus to earth *before* (pre) the beginning of the
Millennium. The word "millennium" is a combination of
two Latin words—*mille annum*—which simply mean
"one thousand years."

A diagram of this viewpoint is presented in Figure
18-1. It divides the future of the world into four periods:
1) the current Church Age; 2) a seven-year period called
the Tribulation; 3) a reign of Christ on earth lasting
1,000 years (the Millennium); and 4) the Eternal State
when the Redeemed will dwell forever with God on a
New Earth.

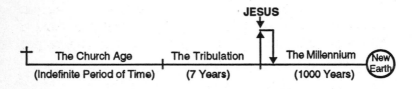

Figure 18-1: Historic Premillennialism

This view is based on a literal interpretation of what
the Bible says will happen in the end times. One of its
distinctive features is that it places the Rapture of the
Church at the end of the Tribulation.

According to this view, the Church will remain on
earth during the Tribulation. At the end of that period,
Jesus will appear in the heavens and the Church will be
caught up to meet Him in the sky. The saints will be
instantly glorified, and then they will immediately
return to the earth to reign with Jesus for a thousand
years.

The Church Fathers

This is virtually the only view of end-time events that existed during the first 300 years of the Church. With one exception, all the Church Fathers who expressed themselves on the topic of prophecy were premillennial until A.D. 400. Justin Martyr, who was born in A.D. 100, went so far in his writings on the subject as to suggest that anyone with a different viewpoint was heretical.

Those today who disagree with this view respond to the near unanimity of the early Church Fathers by saying they were simply wrong in their interpretation of the prophetic Scriptures.

It certainly should be noted that these early Church leaders were not prophetic scholars. They wrote very little on prophecy, and what they wrote was sketchy. Their main concern was not prophecy, but the deity of Jesus, the oneness of God, the practical problems of Church organization, and survival in the face of persecution.

Yet their concept of end-time events should not be dismissed out of hand as crude and primitive, for anyone who has studied the prophetic Scriptures will have to admit that the Church Fathers' viewpoint presents a plain-sense summary of the Bible's teachings about the end times.

The one exception to the consensus opinion among the early Church Fathers was Origen (A.D. 185-254). Origen's approach to all of Scripture was to spiritualize it. He therefore denied the literal meaning of prophecy. He looked upon its language as highly symbolic and expressive of deep spiritual truths rather than of future historical events.

Although Origen could not accept the premillennial viewpoint, he did not develop an alternative. That task fell to one of the greatest of the Church Fathers, Saint

Augustine (A.D. 358-434). He conceived an alternative viewpoint at the end of the fourth century.

Amillennialism

The concept formulated by Augustine is illustrated in Figure 18-2. It is called amillennialism. This strange name derives from the fact that in the Greek language a word is negated by putting the letter "a" in front of it. Thus, *amillennial* literally means "no thousand years."

The term is misleading, however, because most amillennialists do believe in a millennium, but not a literal, earthly one. They argue that the Millennium is the current spiritual reign of Christ over the Church and that it will continue until He returns for His saints. They thus interpret the thousand years as a symbolic period of time.

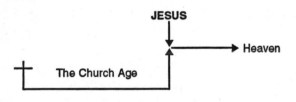

Figure 18-2: Amillennialism

One appealing aspect of the amillennial view is its simplicity. The Church Age comes to a screaming halt as a result of the Rapture of the Church. There is no Tribulation, no literal earthly Millennium, and no eternity on a New Earth. Augustine spiritualized everything, arguing that the kingdom is the Church, the Millennium is the current Church Age, and the New Earth is symbolic language for Heaven.

Augustine's view of end-time events was adopted by the Council of Ephesus in A.D. 431 and has remained

Catholic dogma to this day. It is also the current majority viewpoint among mainline Protestant denominations. In other words, the amillennial viewpoint is the one that is held today by the vast majority of professing Christians.

Postmillennialism

The third view of end-time events, called post-millennialism, did not develop until the mid-seventeenth century, long after the Reformation. The Reformation had little impact on prophetic views because the Reformation leaders had their attention riveted on the questions of biblical authority and justification by faith.

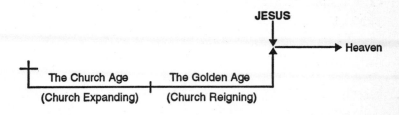

Figure 18-3: Postmillennialism

The postmillennial view was a product of the rationalistic revolution in thinking. It was developed in the mid-1600s by a Unitarian minister named Daniel Whitby. It was immediately dubbed "postmillennialism" because it envisioned a return of Jesus *after* (post) a literal thousand-year reign of the Church over all the earth. This view is illustrated in Figure 18-3.

Postmillennialism spread quickly within the Protestant world, probably for two reasons. First, it gave Protestants an opportunity to differ from the Catholic position. More importantly, it was a theological expression of the prevailing rationalistic philosophy of the age, a philosophy that boldly proclaimed the ability of mankind to build the kingdom of Heaven on earth.

The postmillennial view holds that the Church Age will gradually evolve into a "Golden Age" when the Church will rule over all the world. This will be accomplished through the Christianization of the nations.

To its credit, it can be said that this viewpoint served as a mighty stimulus to missionary efforts during the eighteenth and nineteenth centuries. Missionaries were seized with the vision of speeding up the return of the Lord by preaching the gospel to all the world.

A Sudden Death

By 1900 nearly all segments of Protestant Christianity had adopted the postmillennial viewpoint. But the view was to be quickly dropped.

Postmillennialism died almost overnight with the outbreak of the First World War. The reason, of course, is that this great war undermined one of the fundamental assumptions of the postmillennial viewpoint—the assumption of the inevitability of progress. This had always been a fatal flaw in the postmillennial concept, due mainly to its birth in rationalistic humanism. Its visions of the perfectibility of man and the redemption of society were destroyed by the atrocities of the war.

Another fatal flaw of the postmillennial viewpoint was its lack of a consistent biblical base. To expound the view, it was necessary to literalize some prophecies (those concerning the Millennium) while at the same time spiritualizing other prophecies (the personal presence of the Lord during the Millennium). Also, it was necessary to ignore or explain away the many prophecies in the Bible that clearly state that society is going to get worse rather than better as the time approaches for the Lord's return (Matthew 24:4-24 and 2 Timothy 3:1-5).

The sudden death of postmillennialism left a prophetic vacuum among Protestant groups. Since the postmillennial view was based to a large extent upon a spiritualizing approach to Scripture, most Protestant groups returned to the spiritualized amillennial viewpoint they had abandoned in the 1700s.

However, a new choice of prophetic viewpoint presented itself on the American scene about this same time, and some of the more fundamentalist Protestant groups opted for it. This view was technically called "dispensational premillennialism" because it originated with a group who had been nicknamed "Dispensationalists." I call it the modern premillennial viewpoint.

Modern Premillennialism

The modern premillennial viewpoint crystallized in the early 1800s among a group in England known as the Plymouth Brethren. The view is illustrated in Figure 18-4.

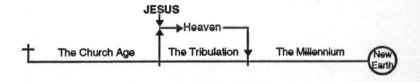

Figure 18-4: Modern Premillennialism

This viewpoint revives the historic premillennial view except for its concept of the Rapture of the Church. The Plymouth Brethren envisioned two future comings of Jesus, one *for* His Church and one *with* His Church. Their concept of the Rapture has since come to be known as the "pre-Tribulation Rapture."

This viewpoint has been attacked as being "too new to be true." But its advocates are quick to point out that

the Bible teaches the principle of "progressive illumination" regarding prophecy (Jeremiah 30:24 and Daniel
12:4). What they mean by this is that the Bible itself
indicates that end-time prophecy will be better understood as the time nears for its fulfillment.

Comparisons

Looking back over these four views of the end times,
we can see some significant differences. But let's not
overlook the similarities.

- All agree that Jesus is coming back for
  His saints.
- All agree that the Redeemed will spend
  eternity in the presence of God.

These two points of agreement are far more important than the many points of disagreement.

Still, the areas of disagreement are significant. Two
of the views (the amillennial and postmillennial) deny
that Jesus will ever manifest His glory before the
nations in a worldwide reign of peace, justice, and righteousness. The postmillennial view also denies the soon
coming of the Lord, for according to this view, the Lord
cannot return until His Church has ruled over the world
for a thousand years.

The key to the differences is the approach to Scripture. If you tend to spiritualize Scripture, you will end
up with an amillennial or a postmillennial viewpoint. If
you tend to accept Scripture for its plain-sense meaning,
you will have a premillennial viewpoint.

A Plea

I urge you to accept the plain-sense meaning of
Scripture. Don't play games with God's Word by spiritualizing it. When you do so, you can make it mean

whatever you want it to mean, but in the process you will lose the true meaning that God intended.

Remember, the First Coming prophecies meant what they said. That should be our guide for interpreting the prophecies of the Second Coming.

19

Amillennial Problems

Are We Really in the Millennium Now?

A friend of mine enrolled in a prominent seminary where the amillennial viewpoint was taught. When he attended his first class in Bible prophecy, the teacher began the class by saying, "There is one fact you must keep in mind about prophetic literature and that is that it never means what it says. So, for example, if you are reading a prophetic verse and it mentions a cow, the only thing you can know for certain about that verse is that the cow is not a cow!"

Such an approach to the Word of God makes a mockery of it. It enables a person to make whatever interpretation he desires. The verse can mean anything he wants it to mean. Yet this is the interpretive principle that serves as the foundation for the amillennial viewpoint.

Augustine's Spiritualizing

The culprit behind this tragedy is Saint Augustine, the man who formulated the amillennial viewpoint around A.D. 400. Augustine "Platonized" the prophetic Scriptures, reading and interpreting the words of the Bible's Hebrew writers as if they had been written by Greek philosophers.

Keep in mind that the Greeks had a creation-negating viewpoint. They viewed the material world as essentially evil. In contrast, the Hebrew view contained in the Scriptures is creation-affirming. To the Hebrew mind, the creation is basically good, even though it has been corrupted by the curse. Thus the psalmist writes: "The heavens are telling of the glory of God; and their expanse is declaring the work of His hands" (Psalm 19:1).

Whereas the Greeks looked toward the dissolution of the universe, the Hebrews yearned for the redemption of the creation. Isaiah dreamed of "the new heavens and the new earth" (Isaiah 66:22), and Paul wrote that the whole creation is longing for its redemption so that it will "be set free from its slavery to corruption" (Romans 8:18-21).

Augustine's Greek worldview would not allow him to accept at face value what the Bible said about end-time events. What the Bible prophesied was too much tied to this world—a future kingdom of Christ on this earth and eternity with God on a New Earth.

Using the spiritualizing approach, Augustine tried to explain away the Tribulation, the Millennium, and the New Earth. The result was the amillennial view-point of end-time events, which holds that the current Church Age will end abruptly with the Rapture of the Church. At that point the Redeemed will be resurrected in spiritual bodies, the unrighteous will be consigned to Hell, the material universe will cease to exist, and the

Redeemed will take up residence with God in an ethereal Heaven.

This view caused a considerable stir when it was originally presented by Saint Augustine because it differed so drastically from the premillennial view of the early Church. The premillennial view envisioned that the Church Age would end with a seven-year period of Tribulation which would be followed by a thousand-year reign of Christ upon the earth. Eternity would be spent in glorified bodies on a New Earth, not in an ethereal Heaven.

The two views are illustrated below for comparison:

1. Historic Premillennial View

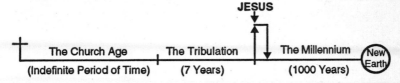

2. Amillennial View

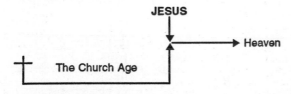

Figure 19-1: Two End-Time Views in Contrast

Augustine's view was adopted quickly by the Catholic Church at the Council of Ephesus in A.D. 431 because it gave enhanced importance to the Church. Based on this new view, the Church could claim that it was the fulfillment of all the kingdom promises in the Bible and that it had a right to rule over the nations.

But Augustine's view raised some serious problems of biblical interpretation.

Where Is the Millennium?

Augustine argued that we are currently in the Millennium! He said the Millennium began at the Cross and would end a thousand years later with the return of Jesus.

When people asked how they could be in the Millennium when there was so much evil in the world, Augustine responded that the level of evil is relative. He said we are in the Millennium because the Holy Spirit is in the world restraining evil. If the Holy Spirit were not here, things would be much worse. Thus, relatively speaking, we are in the Millennium.

For Augustine, the thousand-year length of the Millennium was no problem because he lived in A.D. 400. When the year 1000 passed and the Lord did not return, amillennialists simply spiritualized the number. Since that time they have argued that the number is symbolic and thus represents the period from the Cross to the Second Coming, regardless of how long that may be!

Where Is the Tribulation?

Augustine responded to the question, Where is the Tribulation? by arguing that we are simultaneously in both the Millennium and the Tribulation!

We are in the Millennium because the Holy Spirit is in the world restraining evil, but we are also in the Tribulation because the Church will suffer persecution until the Lord returns.

When it was pointed out that the Bible says the Tribulation will last only seven years, Augustine dismissed the number as symbolic. He argued that the number seven represents a complete period of time, and therefore it (like the number 1,000) represents the period from the Cross to the Second Coming.

Is Satan Bound?

Revelation 20:1-3 reveals that when the Millennium begins, Satan will be bound. This fact forced Augustine to argue that Satan was bound at the Cross. But was he?

Satan was certainly defeated at the Cross due to the power of the resurrection. But that victory at the Cross has not yet been manifested in history in all its aspects. The curse continues. Death stalks the earth. Satan still retains his dominion over the world (1 John 5:19).

The ultimate destruction of Satan is yet future. That's why the Bible speaks of the crushing of Satan as a future event that will take place at the Second Coming of Jesus (Romans 16:20). At that time Satan will be stripped of his authority and bound for a thousand years. At the end of the Millennium, he will be cast into the lake of fire, where he will be tormented forever (Revelation 20:7-10).

Amillennialists often respond to these points by quoting Matthew 28:18, where Jesus said, "All authority has been given to Me in heaven and on earth." But what they overlook is that although Jesus has been *given* all authority, He is not yet *exercising* it. That's why the world is still in such a wretched state.

Jesus is now serving as our High Priest before the throne of God (Hebrews 8:1). When He returns, He will come as the King of kings, and He will begin to exercise in full the authority He won at the Cross (Revelation 19:16). Thus the writer of Hebrews says that although everything has been put in subjection under the feet of Jesus, "we do not yet see all things subjected to him" (Hebrews 2:5-8). In fact, 1 Corinthians 15:23-26 teaches that everything will not be put under the authority of Jesus until the end of His Millennial Reign, when Satan is crushed and death is destroyed.

If Satan is bound now, then he is bound on a very long chain, because he is always nipping at my heels, chewing on my leg, and lunging for my throat! He is portrayed in 1 Peter 5:8 as an "adversary" who "prowls about like a roaring lion, seeking someone to devour." He surely doesn't sound very bound in that passage!

There is certainly a sense in which Satan was limited by the Cross, because since that time believers in Jesus have received the indwelling power of the Spirit, enabling them to be overcomers in their combat with Satan (1 John 5:1-5). But the limitations which the Cross placed on Satan do not constitute the binding of Satan that the Scriptures say will take place at the beginning of the Millennium.

Revelation says Satan will be bound so that he can no longer "deceive the nations" (Revelation 20:3). How can anyone argue that the nations of the world are not deceived today?

Where Are the Resurrections?

Another problem with the amillennial viewpoint is that it does not provide for the two resurrections which the Bible says will occur in the future. These are the resurrections of the just and the unjust (Acts 24:15).

As has been pointed out previously, the premillennial view provides for two resurrections. The first, the resurrection of the righteous, takes place in three stages—the resurrection of Jesus; the resurrection of the Church at the time of the Rapture; and the resurrection of Tribulation martyrs and Old Testament saints at the time of the Lord's Second Coming. The second resurrection, the resurrection of the unrighteous, takes place all at once at the end of the Millennium.

But in the amillennial view, there is only one resurrection. It takes place at the end of the Church Age when history comes to an end. Both the just and the unjust are resurrected at the same time. Where are the two resurrections?

Augustine "solved" this problem by spiritualizing the first resurrection. He said it is a spiritual resurrection that occurs when a person accepts Jesus as Lord and is born again! The second resurrection is a literal one that occurs when everyone is raised from the dead at the Lord's return.

The two resurrections are spoken of specifically in Revelation 20:4-6. The passage says the resurrections are separated by a thousand years. When a person chooses to interpret one of these spiritually and the other literally, he is playing games with words that render them meaningless.

Where Is the New Earth?

Augustine completely spiritualized the concept of a New Earth. His Greek mind-set kept him from accepting the truth that the redeemed will live eternally on a New Earth. He equated the New Earth with Heaven.

From his Greek perspective, it was impossible to mix perfected, holy beings with an evil, material creation. The creation had to cease to exist. Eternity would be spent in an ethereal spirit world.

A Liberal View

To summarize, the amillennial view is based on a spiritualizing approach to Scripture which contends that the Bible does not mean what it says.

This is a consistent view for theological liberals who also spiritualize the creation, the miracles, the virgin birth, and the resurrection of Jesus. But what is astounding is the number of fundamentalists who endorse the amillennial view. In effect, they take the position that the Bible always means what it says unless it is talking about the Second Coming of Jesus!

The Test of Reality

The amillennial view does not stand the test of either the Scriptures or reality. How can anyone truly believe that we are currently living in the Millennium? The Bible says that during the Millennium "the earth will be full of the knowledge of the LORD as the waters cover the sea" (Isaiah 11:9). Does that sound like the world we live in?

Let's not sell God short. When He promised a world characterized by peace, righteousness, and justice (Isaiah 2:2-4), He surely did not have in mind the corrupt world system we are living in now.

To characterize this age as the Millennium is to render meaningless many of the most glorious promises of God. Don't surrender your promises to such a spiritualizing approach.

20

Postmillennialism

Will the Church Convert the World?

I never thought I would live long enough to see the revival of the thoroughly discredited doctrine of postmillennialism. But it has occurred, and it has happened quickly.

The doctrine is sweeping through Christendom today, and strangely enough, it is appealing primarily to two segments at opposite ends of the spectrum—namely, the Charismatics and those with a heritage of Reformed theology.

The doctrine is being presented in new clothes. Although it appears under many different names—Restoration, Reconstruction, New Wave, Latter Rain, and Manifest Sons of God—the two most frequently used titles are Kingdom Now Theology and Dominion Theology.

Characteristics

Regardless of the name, the various groups advocating this confused doctrine hold certain beliefs in common:

1. The Church has replaced Israel, and God has no purpose left for the Jews. Accordingly, many of the proponents are virulently anti-Semitic, even to the point of arguing that the Jewish people are the Antichrist.

2. The Church is destined to take over the world by itself and reign over all the nations for at least 1,000 years.

3. Jesus cannot return for the Church until the Church has completed its reign and is ready to present the kingdom to Him.

Resurrection

As pointed out earlier, postmillennialism died a sudden death when World War I broke out. Since the view is based upon the erroneous assumption of the inevitable progress of Mankind, the First World War killed it because that war rendered it impossible to believe that human progress is inevitable.

Until recently, only one major popular book had been written in this century advocating the postmillennial view. Published in 1957, it was titled *The Millennium*. The author was a Reformed theologian by the name of Loraine Boettner.

When I read this book, I concluded the author probably lived on an isolated island cut off from all news sources. The reason is that he spends a good portion of the book trying to convince the reader that the world really is getting better.

The resurrection of postmillennialism took place in the decade of the eighties, when the market was suddenly flooded with postmillennial books. The two most prolific and influential authors are Earl Paulk and David Chilton.

Two Flavors

Although Paulk and Chilton come to the same erroneous conclusion that the Church will take over the world without the presence of Jesus, their reasoning and methods differ rather drastically.

Paulk's approach is a natural outgrowth of the hyperfaith doctrines that have come to characterize much of the Charismatic movement. Paulk says that Christians are "little gods" with the authority of Christ. We can therefore confess dominion over the earth and, through faith, what we confess will come to pass. Paulk's theology is the one referred to as Kingdom Now.

The other major flavor of the postmillennial revival is called Dominion Theology. Its roots are very different. It is advocated by non-Charismatic, Calvinist theologians.

The philosophical father of Dominion Theology is Rousas John Rushdoony. He has been on the scene for a long time, but his writings are obtuse and have been popular among only a handful of intellectuals. But in the past ten years his theories have been popularized by his son-in-law Gary North of Tyler, Texas, and by David Chilton, a Presbyterian preacher in California.

Dominion Theology differs from Kingdom Now not only in its roots but also in its methods. Kingdom Now supposedly relies on supernatural methods. Believers, as "little gods," assert their godhood by speaking dominion over the nations.

Dominion Theology relies on more traditional methods. The world is to be claimed for Christ through missionary effort and political activism.

Scriptural Arguments

There are three cornerstone Scriptures that are often used to justify the Kingdom Now/Dominion doctrines. The first and foremost is Acts 3:21.

This verse is usually quoted to say, "Jesus must remain in heaven until all things have been restored." Therefore, the argument goes, Jesus cannot return until the Church has emerged triumphant over the world and has restored God's creation through a reign of peace, righteousness, and justice.

The problem with this neat argument is that the verse does not say what the Dominionists quote it to say. Instead, the verse says Jesus must remain in heaven "until the period of restoration of all things." What the verse actually says is therefore drastically different from its subtle Dominionist paraphrase.

The verse means exactly what it says: Jesus must remain in heaven until it is time for the restoration of all things. He will then return and restore the creation and restore God's dominion over the creation, just as prophesied by the Hebrew prophets (see, for example, Isaiah 11:3b-9).

The second Scripture text which Dominionists often point to is Matthew 24:14, which says that the gospel of the kingdom must be preached in the whole world before the end will come. This verse, they say, requires that the world be converted to Christ before He returns.

But this verse does not say that the world must be converted. It says only that the gospel must be preached to all the world.

The Church is preaching the gospel all over the world today, but even so, not every person will hear it until the end of the Tribulation period when an angel of God will be sent forth to proclaim the gospel "to every nation and tribe and tongue and people" (Revelation 14:6). Then Jesus will return in triumph to establish His kingdom from Mount Zion in Jerusalem (Revelation 19 and 20).

A third text sometimes used by the Dominionists is Romans 8:19, which says that "the anxious longing of the creation waits eagerly for the revealing of the sons of God." This is interpreted to mean that the creation will be redeemed as the Church matures, purifies, and spreads its influence over the earth.

But the context of this passage makes it very clear that the verse is talking about the *resurrection* of the saints, not the *maturing* of the saints. The resurrection will reveal those who are truly the sons of God (verse 23). It is at that time that the curse will be lifted from the creation, not before (verse 21).

Unscriptural Conclusions

The lack of scriptural foundation has led the Kingdom Now/Dominion theologians to conclusions that are completely unbiblical. Let's consider these conclusions one by one.

1. *The Jews*—Has God washed His hands of them? The Dominionists claim He has, but Romans 9-11 clearly teaches that the Jews are still the Chosen People of God and that God intends to bring a remnant of them to salvation in Jesus Christ. The disobedience of the Jews has not annulled God's promises to Israel because "the gifts and the calling of God are irrevocable" (Romans 11:29).

2. *The World*—Will the world be converted to Jesus as these revived postmillennialists claim? The Bible teaches that the vast majority of people will always reject the gospel. This is one of the points of the parable of the sower (Matthew 13). Jesus said, "The gate is small, and the way is narrow that leads to life, and few are those who find it" (Matthew 7:14).

3. *The Church*—Is the mission of the Church to convert all nations? Again, that's what the Dominionists claim. But the Bible teaches that it is the responsibility

of the Church to preach the gospel, not to convert the world (Mark 16:15).

4. *The Kingdom*—Does the Church establish a kingdom without a king? This is the view of the Dominionists. The Bible teaches that Jesus will present the kingdom to the Church (Daniel 7:13-14,18,27). The Church is never pictured as presenting the kingdom to Jesus. Furthermore, the Church is always portrayed as reigning with Jesus and not as reigning alone (Revelation 3:21).

5. *Imminency*—The Bible teaches we are to be alert and sober, watching for the imminent return of the Lord for His Church (Matthew 24 and 25). The new postmillennialists deny that the return of Jesus is imminent. In fact, they say He cannot return until the Church has reigned for at least 1,000 years.

6. *Jesus*—Kingdom Now advocates of the revived postmillennialism not only replace Israel with the Church, they also replace Jesus with the Church. Paulk goes so far as to say that the Church is "the ongoing incarnation of Christ." This is blasphemy. There is only one Christ, and that is Jesus of Nazareth. The focus of God's plan of redemption for all of His creation is not the Church; it is Jesus (Hebrews 1). And any doctrine that causes us to take our eyes off the Lord is profoundly false.

The Second Coming

One of the most incredible claims of Kingdom Now/ Dominion eschatology is that the Second Coming of Christ occurred in the first century!

The new postmillennialists are forced to take this position in order to explain away all the prophecies in Revelation concerning the return of Jesus. They argue that all these prophecies were fulfilled in the destruction of Jerusalem in A.D. 70.

They view the Jews as the Antichrist. The siege of Jerusalem by Roman troops under Titus is pictured as the Tribulation, and the destruction of Jerusalem is seen as the Second Coming of Jesus in wrath.

This interpretation, of course, requires the book of Revelation to have been written before A.D. 70. But the internal evidence of the book regarding the Roman Empire and the external testimony of the Church Fathers both point to a date of authorship around A.D. 95, 25 years after the destruction of Jerusalem.

The type of widespread Roman persecution of the Church that is described in Revelation did not occur until the reign of Domitian (A.D. 81-96). One of the Church Fathers, Irenaeus (A.D. 120-202), wrote that the book of Revelation was authored by the apostle John "towards the end of Domitian's reign." Irenaeus was discipled by Polycarp (A.D. 70-155), who in turn had been discipled directly by John himself.

The evidence is simply overwhelming that the book of Revelation was written after the destruction of Jerusalem. This fact alone completely destroys the whole foundation of Dominionist eschatology.

The preposterous concept that the Second Coming of Christ occurred in A.D. 70 is reminiscent of two fellows in the time of Paul—Hymenaeus and Philetus—who argued that the resurrection had already taken place (2 Timothy 2:17-18). Paul dismissed their claim as "worldly and empty chatter" that will "lead to further ungodliness" (2 Timothy 2:16). We would do well to follow Paul's advice regarding the Dominionist claim that the Second Coming occurred in the first century.

A New Age of Deception

We are living in the season of the Lord's return. All the signs point to the fact that Jesus will return for His Church at any moment. What more could Satan wish for at this time than the rebirth of a doctrine that destroys the imminency of the Lord's return and gets people's eyes focused not on Jesus but on the world and the creation of a worldwide kingdom?

This deception is preparing people for the emergence of the Antichrist, for the Bible teaches that the only worldwide kingdom that will be established before the return of Jesus will be the apostate kingdom of the Antichrist, a kingdom that will be established in the name of religion (Revelation 13).

A Warning

Every time the Church has sought political power, it has ended up being corrupted by the political system. This happened when the Church was wed with the Roman Empire, leading to the spiritual darkness of the Middle Ages.

The deadest churches in the world today are the state churches of Europe. They have the form of religion, but they have denied its power (2 Timothy 3:5). They have political power, but they do not have the power of God's Spirit.

Do not be deceived by those who urge the Church to change the world through the pursuit of political power. It is true that a day will come when the Church will reign over all the world, but that reign will be conducted in person by Jesus through His glorified saints. A perfect kingdom requires a perfect king ruling through perfected subjects.

21

Matthew 24

History or Prophecy?

Is Matthew 24 history or prophecy? This is a crucial
prophetic question. The passage clearly portrays a
period of intense tribulation that will precede the Second Coming of Jesus. Has this terrible period of tribulation already occurred, or is it yet to occur? Is it past or
future? History or prophecy?

Two Conflicting Views

The premillennialist viewpoint, both historic and
modern, holds this passage to be predictive, yet-to-be-
fulfilled sometime in the near future. According to the
premillennial view, the return of Jesus will be immediately preceded by a period of great, worldwide tribulation that will particularly focus on the Jewish people.

The majority viewpoint of Christendom, both Catholic and Protestant, is the amillennial view. This view

179

spiritualizes Bible prophecy and concludes that there will be no future Tribulation or Millennium. Amillennialists argue that we are simultaneously experiencing both the Tribulation and the Millennium right now and have been doing so since the Cross.

Although postmillennialists would argue that the Millennium is still future, they would agree with the amillennialists that Matthew 24 was fulfilled in the first-century destruction of Jerusalem. They conclude, therefore, that there will be no future Tribulation.

Matthew 24 thus emerges as a key prophetic passage. Those who spiritualize prophecy (amillennialists and postmillennialists) argue that it has been fulfilled in history and therefore reject the idea that it points to a period of severe tribulation immediately preceding the return of Jesus. Those who interpret prophecy more literally (premillennialists) contend that the passage awaits fulfillment. They believe it definitely points to a period of tribulation before the Lord returns.

Inconsistent Interpretation

The interpretation given to Matthew 24 by amillennialists and postmillennialists is very interesting. It is also very inconsistent with the way they interpret other prophecies.

Instead of spiritualizing it, like they do most prophetic passages, they accept it to be literal prophecy. But they argue that it is prophecy that was fulfilled 40 years after it was spoken, when the Roman legions under Titus destroyed Jerusalem in A.D. 70 and scattered the Jews across the world.

So, what about our central question? Is Matthew 24 history or prophecy? Is it past or future? Was it fulfilled in A.D. 70 or is it yet to occur?

I believe Matthew 24 was *pre-filled* in type in the destruction of Jerusalem in A.D. 70 and is therefore yet to be *fulfilled* in history. And I think I can prove that from the passage itself.

Daniel's Prophecy

To begin with, consider verse 15. It says the period of intense persecution of the Jews will begin when "the abomination of desolation," spoken of by Daniel, is seen "standing in the holy place."

We have no historical record of such an event taking place in A.D. 70. Unlike the Greek tyrant, Antiochus Epiphanes, who desecrated the Temple's holy place in 168 B.C. by erecting within it an altar to Zeus, Titus took no such action in A.D. 70 before he destroyed the city and the Temple.

The Intensity of the Tribulation

The second point to note is found in verse 21. It says that the period of Jewish persecution that will follow the desecration of the Temple will be the most intense in all of history, "since the beginning of the world until now, nor ever shall [be]."

These words were not fulfilled in A.D. 70. The persecution that the Jews experienced under Titus was severe, but it pales in comparison to what the Jews suffered during the Nazi Holocaust of World War II.

Josephus says the Romans killed a million Jews in the A.D. 70 A.D. siege of Jerusalem. Historians are convinced that this number is greatly exaggerated. But even if it is true, it is still nothing compared to the six million Jews who perished at the hands of the Nazis.

Furthermore, the prophet Zechariah tells us that during the end times a total of two-thirds of the Jewish people will die during a period of unparalleled calamity (Zechariah 13:8-9). In other words, there is a period of Jewish persecution yet to occur that will exceed even the horrors of the Nazi Holocaust.

Consider verse 21 again: "Then there will be a great tribulation, such as has not occurred since the beginning of the world until now, nor ever shall." Did Jesus mean what He said or not? Surely this is not an example of hyperbole—of exaggeration to make a point. Everything in the passage fairly screams that we are to take Jesus' words literally.

The conclusion is inescapable. The tribulation experienced by the Jews in A.D. 70 was not the greatest "since the beginning of the world until now, nor ever shall [be]."

The Severity of the Tribulation

The third piece of evidence is found in verse 22. Jesus says that the period of "great tribulation" (verse 21) that He is talking about will be so severe that all life will cease unless the period is cut short.

You and I live in the only generation in history when these words could be literally fulfilled. There was no possibility in A.D. 70 that the siege of Jerusalem would lead to the extinction of all life. But that is a very real threat today due to the development and deployment of nuclear weapons.

The best-selling book of 1982, *The Fate of the Earth*, proved that if there is ever an all-out nuclear exchange between the United States and Russia, *all* life on earth will cease to exist.

The Proximity of the Tribulation

The fourth clue that Matthew 24 is yet to be fulfilled is found in verse 29. It says the Lord will return "immediately after the tribulation of those days." How can we escape the impact of the word "immediately"? I don't think we can. It clearly ties the preceding events to the immediate time of Jesus' return.

As I pointed out in the previous chapter, some amillennialists and postmillennialists have tried to deal with this problem in a fanciful way by claiming that the Second Coming of Jesus actually occurred in A.D. 70! Of course, that is ludicrous, but it shows the extent to which some people will go to try to make Scripture conform to a particular doctrine.

The Context of the Tribulation

The final evidence that Matthew 24 was not fulfilled in A.D. 70 is to be found in verses 32-35, where Jesus says that all the things He has spoken of concerning the Tribulation will be fulfilled during the generation that sees the "fig tree" reblossom. Here is the key to the timing of the prophecy's fulfillment.

What is the "fig tree"? Think back for a moment to what had happened the day before. Jesus had put a curse on a barren fig tree (Matthew 21:18-19), causing it to wither. It was a prophetic sign that God would set the Jewish nation aside because of their spiritual barrenness—that is, their refusal to accept Jesus as their Messiah. The fig tree is a symbol of the nation of Israel (Jeremiah 24:1-10; Hosea 9:10; Joel 1:7; Luke 13:6-9).

Now, the next day, Jesus calls the fig tree to mind and says, "Watch it. When it reblossoms, all these things will happen."

The setting aside of Israel occurred in A.D. 70. The reblossoming took place in 1948, when the nation of Israel was reestablished.

A Fact to Ponder

Matthew 24 is not history. The terrible events of A.D. 70 were a classic pre-fillment in type of the ultimate fulfillment that will occur immediately before the Lord returns.

Matthew 24 is prophecy yet to be fulfilled. It is going to be fulfilled soon, for Israel has been regathered, the nation has been reestablished, and the nations of the world are coming together against the Jewish state. The wrath of God is about to fall. We are on the threshold of the Great Tribulation.

As you ponder this reality, are you ready for it? Have you received Jesus as your Lord and Savior? The Bible says that if you put your faith in Jesus, you need not fear the wrath of God, for "having now been justified by His blood, we shall be saved from the wrath of God through Him" (Romans 5:9).

22

The Millennium

Why Bother?

When I first began studying Bible prophecy, the question, What purpose would the Millennium serve? really bothered me. The Word clearly taught that the Lord is coming back to this earth to reign for a thousand years. But I kept asking, Why?

I have since discovered that most amillennialists feel that same way. "Why," they will ask, "would the Lord want to come back to this rotten world? What could possibly be His purpose in returning to this world to reign for a thousand years? Why does the Lord or the world need a Millennium?"

My study of the Word has led me to conclude that God has several vitally important purposes for the Millennium.

Promises to the Jews

The first reason there must be a Millennium is that God has made promises to the Jews which He will fulfill during that time.

God has promised that He will gather to the land of Israel the remnant of Jews who accept Jesus as their Messiah at the end of the Tribulation (Ezekiel 36:22-28 and Zechariah 10:6-9). He will pour out His Spirit upon this remnant (Isaiah 32:15; 44:3), greatly expand their numbers and their land (Ezekiel 36:10-11; 48:1-29), and make them the prime nation in all the world (Isaiah 60-62).

They will serve as an object lesson of the grace and mercy which God bestows upon those who turn to Him in repentance:

> It will come about that just as you were a curse among the nations, O house of Judah and house of Israel, so I will save you that you may become a blessing (Zechariah 8:13).

Zechariah says the blessings of God upon the Jewish remnant will be so great in those days that "ten men from all the nations will grasp the garment of a Jew saying, 'Let us go with you, for we have heard that God is with you'" (Zechariah 8:23).

Promises to the Church

A second reason for the Millennium relates to a promise which God has made to the Church. God has promised that the Redeemed in Christ will reign over all the nations of the world.

This promise was given through the prophet Daniel in the following words:

> Then the sovereignty, the dominion, and the greatness of all the kingdoms under the whole heaven will be given to the people of the saints of the Highest One; His kingdom

will be an everlasting kingdom, and all the
dominions will serve and obey Him (Daniel
7:27).

In the New Testament, Paul repeated the same
promise in the simplest of terms: "If we endure, we shall
also reign with Him" (2 Timothy 2:12). Jesus affirmed
the promise in His letter to the church at Thyatira when
He wrote:

And he who overcomes, and he who keeps
My deeds until the end, to him I will give
authority over the nations; and he shall
rule them with a rod of iron (Revelation
2:26-27).

When John was taken to Heaven for a visit to the
throne room of God, he heard a heavenly host singing a
song that contained the following verse: "And Thou has
made them [the Redeemed] to be a kingdom and priests
to our God; and they will reign upon the earth" (Revelation 5:10).

This promise to the Church of worldwide dominion is
going to be fulfilled during the Millennium. That is
what Jesus was referring to in the Sermon on the Mount
when He said, "Blessed are the gentle, for they shall
inherit the earth" (Matthew 5:5).

Jesus will reign as king of the world from Mount
Zion in Jerusalem (Isaiah 24:23 and Zechariah 14:9).
The Redeemed, in their glorified bodies, will help Him
with His reign by serving worldwide as administrators,
judges, and spiritual tutors to those who enter the kingdom in the flesh—and to their children (Jeremiah 3:15;
Daniel 7:18,27; Luke 19:11-17).

Promises to the Nations

God has promised that a time will come when the
nations will be provided with their greatest dream—

namely, worldwide peace. This has been an international dream since the beginning of time, but it has proved to be impossibly elusive.

Peace conference after peace conference has been held. Multiple treaties have been signed. World organizations have been formed. Yet war continues to ravage the nations.

God has promised to give Mankind and the earth a rest from its wars. But that peace will not come until the Prince of Peace returns. Only then will the nations "hammer their swords into plowshares, and their spears into pruning hooks." Only then will we realize the dream of a world where "nation will not lift up sword against nation, and never again will they learn war" (Isaiah 2:4).

God has promised that He will flood the earth with peace, righteousness, justice, and holiness: "The earth will be full of the knowledge of the LORD as the waters cover the sea" (Isaiah 11:9). Even the bells on the horses' bridles and the pots in the kitchens will bear the inscription "Holy to the Lord" (Zechariah 14:20,21).

These glorious promises of peace and rest and righteousness will be fulfilled during the Millennium.

Promises to the Creation

God has also made promises to His creation which He will fulfill during the Millennium.

God has promised to remove the curse which He placed upon the creation due to the sin of Man. He has promised to deliver the creation from its bondage to decay and to restore it to its original beauty, balance, and peace (Romans 8:18-23).

The carnivorous animals will become herbivorous (Isaiah 11:6). The deadly animals will cease to be poisonous (Isaiah 11:8-9). The plant kingdom will flourish and produce bountifully (Isaiah 35 and Ezekiel 34:25-31).

The land of Israel will be so radically transformed that visitors will proclaim in amazement: "This desolate land has become like the garden of Eden" (Ezekiel 36:35).

Promises to Jesus

The most important reason of all for the Millennium is that God is going to use it to fulfill promises that He has made to His Son.

God has promised Jesus that He will be glorified in history to compensate in part for His humiliation in history. The Bible says point-blank that Jesus will return to manifest His glory (Isaiah 24:23; 66:18-19; 2 Thessalonians 1:7-10).

God also has promised that He will give Jesus dominion over all the world and that He will reign over the nations from Mount Zion in Jerusalem (Isaiah 2:2-4; Daniel 7:13-14; Zechariah 14:1-9).

Psalm 2 presents a good summary of these promises. It begins by surveying the rebellion of the world's political leaders against God and His Son, referred to in the passage as "His Anointed" (verses 1-2). It describes their contempt for the Lord (verse 3).

But the psalm says that God sits in the heavens and laughs and scoffs at them because He has appointed a day of reckoning when He will "terrify them in His fury" (verse 5). That will be the day when He installs Jesus as "King upon Zion" (verse 6).

Jesus then speaks and tells of the promise that His Father has made to Him:

I will surely tell of the decree of the LORD: He said to Me, "Thou art My Son, today I have begotten Thee. Ask of Me, and I will surely give the nations as Thine inheritance, and the very ends of the earth as Thy possession. Thou shalt break them with a rod of iron" (Psalm 2:7-9).

Jesus is currently a "king-in-waiting." Like King David, who had to wait many years after he was anointed before he became king of Israel, Jesus has been anointed King of kings and Lord and lords, but He has not yet begun to rule.

He is currently serving as our High Priest before the throne of God (Hebrews 8:1). He is waiting for His Father's command to return and claim all the kingdoms of this world (Hebrews 2:5-9 and Revelation 19:11-16).

A Final Reason

There is one other important purpose for the Millennium: God will use it to prove to Man once and for all that humanism is totally bankrupt.

All humanists, regardless of their political or theological labels, agree that the source of evil in the world is external to Man. They view evil as rooted in the corruption of society. They believe that the solution to all Man's problems can be found in societal reform.

Take, as an example, their attitude toward crime. They believe society is the root cause of crime. All we have to do to eliminate crime, they argue, is to provide people with a guaranteed job that will supply them with sufficient income so that they will be able to live in a nice suburb.

But such reforms do not transform the basic nature of people. In the ghetto a man will pay 25 dollars for a prostitute. In the suburb he will chase his neighbor's wife. In the ghetto he will throw a rock through a window and steal a TV set. In the suburb he will put on his three-piece suit, go to the office, manipulate the computer, and embezzle a million dollars.

You do not change people's basic nature by changing their environment. Changing their environment simply converts them into more sophisticated sinners.

The humanist view is absolutely contrary to Scripture. The Word of God teaches that the source of evil is rooted within Man's fallen nature, and that it is Man, and not society, which needs to be changed (Genesis 8:21; Jeremiah 17:9-10; Mark 7:20-23). The Word also teaches that the only way this change can take place is through the work of the Holy Spirit within a person who has put his faith in Jesus.

God is going to prove this point by using the Millennium like a great experimental laboratory. He is going to place Mankind in a perfect environment of peace and prosperity for a thousand years. Satan will be bound. Righteousness will abound.

Yet at the end, when Satan is released, most people will rally to him when he calls the nations to rebellion against Jesus (Revelation 20:7-10). The Millennium will prove that what Man needs is not a new society but a new heart.

Essential to the Master Plan

The Millennium is essential for the fulfillment of all the promises that God has made to the Jews, the Church, the nations, and the creation.

It is also essential to His determination to prove that the source of all evil is the fallen nature of Man, not the corruption of society, and that the only hope for this world is Jesus, not political reform.

Most important, the Millennium is essential to God's purpose in glorifying His Son. He is going to manifest the glory of Jesus before His redeemed saints and before all the nations of the world.

> All the ends of the earth will remember and turn to the LORD, and all the families of the nations will worship before Thee. For the kingdom is the LORD's, and He rules over the nations.... Posterity will serve Him; it will be told of the Lord to the coming generation. They will come and will declare His

righteousness to a people who will be born,
that He has performed it (Psalm 22:27-31).

God's Faithfulness

The Creator of this universe is a covenant-making
God who is faithful to all His promises. He cannot lie
(Hebrews 6:18). He cannot forget a promise (Deuteronomy 4:31). He is faithful even when we are unfaithful
(2 Timothy 2:13).

Just as He fulfilled all the promises related to the
First Coming of His Son, He is going to fulfill all those
that relate to the Second Coming, including the promise
of a millennial reign.

Many in the Church may be ignorant of His unfulfilled promises. Others may have forgotten them. But
God has not. He intends to fulfill every one of them.

We are privileged to live in a time when we can
witness God orchestrating the events of this world to
the fulfillment of all the promises in His master plan.

> Ascribe greatness to our God!
> The Rock! His work is perfect.
> For all His ways are just;
> A God of faithfulness and without injustice,
> Righteous and upright is He (Deuteronomy
> 32:3b-4).

PART
4

Prophetic Signs

"But you, brethren, are not in darkness, that the day [of the Lord] should overtake you like a thief."

—1 Thessalonians 5:4

23

The Second Coming

Can We Know
When Jesus Will Return?

Can we know when Jesus will return? The answer is yes and no. No, we cannot know the date. Yes, we can know the season.

The reason we can know the season is because the Bible is full of signs which will signal the season of the Lord's return, and we are told to watch for them. These signs are found in both the Old and New Testaments, and there are a great number of them.

For example, one out of every 25 verses in the New Testament specifically covers the Second Coming. But what is not so well known is the fact that there are over 500 prophecies in the Old Testament which also relate to the Second Coming of Christ.

In addition to the Major and Minor Prophets, the Psalms are full of messianic prophecies regarding the Lord's return. In fact, Psalm 2 is one of the most important Second Coming prophecies in the Bible.

A great variety of signs are revealed in these Scriptures. There are signs of nature, spiritual signs, signs that relate to the nature of society, international political signs, signs of technology, and signs that concern the Jewish people.

An Area of Ignorance

Many Christians have ignored the study of these signs because they believe that since "Jesus is coming like a thief in the night," it is a waste of time to try to interpret the signs to anticipate the time of His coming.

When I was growing up, this phrase was used as a big put-down. If anyone got excited about the Lord's return, someone would immediately try to stifle his or her enthusiasm by asserting, "He's coming like a thief." That meant shut up about it because there is nothing you can know about it.

It is true that Jesus said He would come like a thief in the night (Matthew 24:42-43). But Paul later explained that Jesus meant this statement for non-believers, not for Christians.

Paul's Revelation

Paul makes this point in his first letter to the Thessalonians. In chapter 5 he says that although Jesus is coming back like a thief in the night, there is no reason for His return to surprise any Christian (1 Thessalonians 5:4). Why not? Because, as Paul puts it, "You, brethren, are not in darkness, that the day should overtake you like a thief; for you are all sons of light and sons of day" (1 Thessalonians 5:4-5).

What does Paul mean by this seemingly enigmatic statement? I think he was referring to the fact that when we accept Jesus as our Savior, we are given the indwelling presence of the Holy Spirit (Romans 5:5). Through the Spirit we receive the power to become spiritually enlightened. John says in 1 John 2:27 that the

Holy Spirit can illuminate our minds to understand the Word of God.

In other words, Paul is saying in 1 Thessalonians 5 that we can know the season of the Lord's return because we have been given spiritual discernment through the gift of the Holy Spirit.

But the spiritual discernment Paul is talking about is not gained by praying for God to zap us with it. It comes through the guidance of the Holy Spirit as we study God's Word. And because the study of prophecy has been so sorely ignored, many Christians are going to be surprised by the return of Christ.

Jesus' Concept

In Matthew 24, Jesus compared the signs of His return to the signs of a pregnancy. Think of it this way: You may not know the date when a pregnant woman is to deliver, but sooner or later, as you watch the development of her pregnancy, you will think to yourself, *That baby is going to be born soon!* Why? You can tell by looking.

Jesus said the signs pointing to His return would be like "birth pangs" (Matthew 24:8). Any mother who has given birth knows what Jesus meant by this remark. As the time nears for His return, the signs will increase in frequency and intensity, just like birth pangs. For example, there will be more earthquakes and they will be more intense.

This is a crucial point that is usually overlooked. People often scoff at the signs by saying, "There have *always* been wars and rumors of wars and earthquakes and famines." Yes, there have always been such calamities—but they are now increasing in frequency and intensity, just as Jesus prophesied.

Peter's View

Peter tells us that one of the signs of the end times will be an outbreak of scoffing at the idea of the return of

Jesus (2 Peter 3:3-4). We live in such times. The tragedy is that so much of the scoffing comes from Christians who are ignorant of God's Prophetic Word.

Peter also tells us that God does not wish that anyone should perish but that all should be brought to repentance (2 Peter 3:9). That's why God has given us so many signs to watch for. As the prophet Amos put it: "Surely the LORD God does nothing unless He reveals His secret counsel to His servants the prophets" (Amos 3:7).

Jesus' Warning

Jesus condemned the religious leaders of His time because they refused to heed the signs of the times. On one occasion they came to Him and asked Him to perform a miracle to prove He was the Messiah. Jesus rebuked them severely. "Do you know how to discern the appearance of the sky," He said, "but cannot discern the signs of the times?" (Matthew 16:3).

Jesus was trying to point out that although these men could predict the weather by reading the signs of nature, they could not interpret His significance by reading the signs of God's Word.

What did Jesus mean by the "signs of the times"? He was referring to the fact that the Hebrew Scriptures contain more than 300 prophecies about His First Coming.

These same Scriptures contain many more signs about the Second Coming of Jesus, and those signs point to *this* day and age as the season of our Lord's return.

Another Warning

But as we heed the signs of the Lord's soon return, we need to keep in mind another warning that Jesus gave. With regard to the exact date of His return He said, "Of that day and hour no one knows, not even the

angels of heaven, nor the Son, but the Father alone"
(Matthew 24:36).

As we get nearer to the day of the Lord's return,
Satan will motivate people to set exact dates. Many of
these will be very sincere people who will be sincerely
deceived.

Satan loves date-setting. It focuses people's attention on a date rather than on the Lord. It draws the
ridicule of the secular press. It leads to bitter disillusion-
ment as people put their faith in the date and then are
severely disappointed when the date comes and passes
without the Lord appearing.

Date-setting turns people off to God's Prophetic
Word. It has the same effect as a person constantly
crying "Wolf!" when there is no wolf. People finally
start disbelieving in wolves—and suddenly the pack is
upon them.

Likewise, people who have been disappointed or
embarrassed by fixing their hope on a specific date often
react to the debacle by turning off to prophecy. Then,
when a responsible prophecy teacher comes along teaching we can know the *season*, they respond with skepti-
cism, saying, "I've heard that line before, and you're not
going to make a sucker out of me again!"

Knowing the Season

Knowing the season does not mean knowing the
date. A season is a general period of time.

A few years ago after I had preached a sermon trying
to prove that we are living in the season of the Lord's
return, an elderly man came up to me and said, "That
was a pretty good sermon, young man, but I've got news
for you. You see, when I was a boy, my pastor preached
the very same sermon during World War I."

What that man did not realize is that his boyhood
pastor was right on target, for—as we shall see in the

next chapter—we have been in the season of the Lord's return ever since World War I began.

Noah preached for 120 years that people were living in the season of the pouring out of God's wrath. People laughed and scoffed at him. Can you imagine what they must have been saying about him 50 years into his ministry? "That crazy old fool Noah is a one-issue-obsessionist! He's been preaching the same message for 50 years and nothing has happened yet!" Some of them laughed until they could tread water no longer.

God's Character

God is incredibly patient. David expressed it this way in Psalm 103:8: "The LORD is compassionate and gracious, slow to anger and abounding in lovingkindness." Peter tells us why: "The Lord is . . . patient toward you, not wishing for any to perish but for all to come to repentance" (2 Peter 3:9).

This is precisely the reason that God gives us so many signs to mark the season of His Son's return. You see, Jesus is returning in incredible wrath (Revelation 6:12-17). He is coming to pour out the wrath of God upon those who have rejected the love, grace, and mercy of God.

Because Jesus is returning in wrath, God is obligated by His character to warn us. The Bible teaches that God never pours out His wrath without warning. God is not interested in catching anyone by surprise with the return of His Son.

But tragically, most will be surprised, even shocked, because they will fail to heed the signs of the times. The Word says that the political leaders of the world will cry out for the rocks of the mountains to fall upon them (Revelation 6:15-16).

Those who are surprised will have no one to blame but themselves. God is shouting from the heavens in many different ways that the time is fast approaching when His Son will return to judge and wage war (Revelation 19:11).

A Challenge

Jesus is coming soon. All the signs point to it. He is "right at the door" (Matthew 24:33), and for all those who have studied God's Prophetic Word, He will return as their "blessed hope" (Titus 2:13) and not as a thief in the night.

Are you ready? If Jesus were to return today, would He come as your Blessed Hope or would He catch you unprepared?

The choice is yours. The time is short. God is patient, but He will not be mocked. Here's how the prophet Nahum put it: "The LORD is slow to anger and great in power, and the LORD will by no means leave the guilty unpunished" (Nahum 1:3).

24

The Signs of the Times

*Significant Pointers
or Flights of Fantasy?*

In Hebrews 10:25 we are told that we are to be "encouraging one another; and all the more, as you see the day drawing near." The context is the Second Coming of Jesus.

This passage makes it clear that we can know the season of the Lord's return—that tangible things will be visible to alert us to the Lord's soon return. What are those things? What are the signs the Bible tells us to watch for?

There are a great number and variety of these signs. In fact, there are so many that it is difficult to get a handle on them. They tend to overwhelm you.

The best way I have found to get a grasp on them is to group them into several broad categories. Let's take a look at them in that manner.

The Signs of Nature

The signs pertaining to nature have gained the least respect. Often when I point to these signs, people react by saying, "You've got to be kidding!"

The problem is twofold. First, people are prone to think, "There have always been earthquakes, volcanic eruptions, hurricanes, and famine. So, what else is new?" As I pointed out in the previous chapter, these people are either ignorant of or have ignored the fact that Jesus said these natural signs would be like "birth pangs" and would thus increase in frequency and intensity as the time draws near for His return.

The second problem is more philosophical. We are a very rationalistic people, and as such we tend to be skeptical of the supernatural. If we can't see it, weigh it, and measure it, we can't accept its existence. Yet the Bible teaches there is a whole realm of reality that is not normally perceptible to the senses—the realm of the supernatural, which includes angels and demons (Ephesians 6:10-12).

Because we are so rationalistic, we tend to scoff at the idea that God would speak to us through signs of nature. But the Bible affirms this over and over. The Old Testament prophets repeatedly pointed to signs of nature and claimed that they indicated the judgment of God or His impending wrath.

The book of Joel is a classic example of this point. The book begins with the prophet pointing to a locust invasion that has stripped the land barren. He declares that this is no accident of nature or just bad luck. Rather, the locusts were sent by the Lord as a warning, calling them to repentance. And the prophet makes it clear that if they do not heed the warning, God will send something worse than the locusts—namely, a foreign army.

God has always spoken through signs of nature, just as He did when He put a special light in the heavens to mark the birth of Jesus. Likewise, on the day Jesus was crucified, Jerusalem experienced a great earthquake and three hours of unusual darkness. On the day Jesus returns, we are told that the greatest earthquake in history will shake the world. Every mountain will be lowered, every valley will be lifted, and every island will be moved (Revelation 16:17-21).

It is no wonder that Jesus told us to watch for "famines and earthquakes" (Matthew 24:7) and for plagues and "signs from heaven" (Luke 21:11).

Nor is it any wonder that a glance at the statistics in a world almanac will confirm that all of these natural calamities have been increasing in frequency and intensity in this century. As earthquakes continue to shake our West Coast, as scientists make startling new discoveries in the heavens, as famine sweeps Africa, and as AIDS stalks the world, we need to get serious about the signs of nature.

God is speaking. Are you listening?

The Signs of Society

Jesus said He would return at a time when society would resemble "the days of Noah" (Matthew 24:37).

The Old Testament tells us that Noah's age was one of wickedness and violence because the thoughts of men's hearts were continually focused on evil (Genesis 6:5-13). The New Testament reveals even more about the degraded nature of Noah's society.

Romans 1:18-32 gives a chilling description of a society wallowing in immorality. In this passage, Paul says the root cause of all the problems is man's rejection of God: "They exchanged the truth of God for a lie, and worshiped and served the creature rather than the Creator" (Romans 1:25). In other words, they put their faith in Man, giving their allegiance to humanism, the religion of Satan.

Paul says that because they turned their backs on God, He removed some of His restraints on evil and "gave them over in the lusts of their hearts to impurity" (Romans 1:24). The result was an outbreak of sexual sin in the form of fornication and adultery.

When they continued in their idolatry and immorality, God removed His remaining restraints on evil and "gave them over to degrading passions" (Romans 1:26). The result was an epidemic of homosexuality which produced woeful diseases, for men received "in their own persons the due penalty of their error" (Romans 1:27).

As the homosexual plague gained momentum, the society slipped quickly into a cesspool of wickedness. People were filled with greed, envy, deceit, hatred, arrogance, and malice. These attitudes were reflected in a growing tide of unrighteous acts. Slander, rebellion, and violence increased (Romans 1:28-31).

Paul speaks in the first chapter of Romans as a historian, telling us what the days of Noah were like. In 2 Timothy 3:1-5 he speaks as a prophet, using almost the identical language of Romans to tell us what the society of the end times will be like. In doing so, he confirms the statement of Jesus that He will return at a time when society has gone full circle, returning to the depravity of Noah's day.

Paul says that the society of the end times will be characterized by great stress (2 Timothy 3:1). It will be a society in which Man will love three things: self, money, and pleasure (2 Timothy 3:2-4). What Paul identifies here is the religion, the god, and the lifestyle of the end-time society.

The religion will be the same as in the times of Noah. It will be humanism, the love of self. Whenever humanism is the religion, the god is always materialism, the love of money. And when materialism is the god, the lifestyle is always hedonism, the love of pleasure.

These three satanic loves—self, money, and pleasure—combine to produce a fourth characteristic called nihilism. It is the payoff. We reap what we sow (Galatians 6:7), and the harvest of humanism, materialism, and hedonism is nihilism—or despair.

Paul describes the resulting despair in graphic terms: "Men will be...boastful, arrogant, revilers, disobedient to parents, ungrateful, unholy, unloving, irreconcilable, malicious gossips, without self-control, brutal, haters of good, treacherous, reckless, conceited" (2 Timothy 3:2-4).

Does it sound familiar? It sounds like the evening news to me.

We call ourselves a Christian nation, but our predominant religion is really humanism. Humanists control the Congress, the judiciary, the presidency, the bureaucracy, and the schools.

We are a nation of materialists who worship the dollar. Greed is the motivating force of big labor, big business, big government, big religion, and big sports.

And do I really need to say anything about our hedonistic lifestyle? "If it feels good, do it!" is the philosophy of our age.

What's worse is that we are exporting our pagan values and lifestyle to the rest of the world through our degrading television programs and movies. The American dream of money, sex, and power has become the world's dream.

And we are reaping what we have sown. Our society wallows in despair as people seek to fill the vacuum in their lives with drugs, alcohol, sex, and violence. Prophecy is being fulfilled before our very eyes—and Jesus is coming soon.

The Spiritual Signs

There are numerous spiritual signs that we are to watch for, both negative and positive ones.

The negative ones are very negative indeed. They include such things as the appearance of false Christs and their cultic groups (Matthew 24:5,11,24), the apostasy of the professing church (2 Timothy 3:5), the persecution of faithful Christians (Luke 21:12-19), and an outbreak of Satanism (1 Timothy 4:1).

We are in the midst of the fulfillment of all these prophecies. The cults began their major assault on the Church with the founding of the Mormon Church in the nineteenth century. Since that time, the cults have multiplied profusely to the point that today they are operating all over the world, preaching a false Jesus and deceiving millions.

Meanwhile, much of mainline Christianity wallows in apostasy. Many of the old-line denominations have rejected the authority of the Scriptures and are now ordaining homosexuals and preaching New Age philosophy. Some Charismatic groups have rejected the true gospel for a Pollyanna gospel that promises health, wealth, and power. Others have decided that preaching the Word is too offensive to the world, and so they are spooning out a positive-thinking pabulum that is designed to make people comfortable with their sins.

True Christians—those who live their faith, speak out against ungodliness, and stand for righteousness— are being submitted to increasing persecution. Their rights are being denied in schools. They are discriminated against in the workplace in both hiring and promotion. They are mocked by the entertainment media. Their churches are increasingly harassed by zoning codes and vandals.

Satan is on the prowl. He knows Bible prophecy, and he knows his time is short. He is attacking the Church with a vengeance. He has also gone public, and the consequent outbreak of Satanism is something to behold. It is pervasive. Satanic themes dominate books, movies, television programs, and music. People are enthralled with astrology, numerology, transcendental meditation, channeling, crystal-gazing, and many other manifestations of occultic entrapment.

I warned you that the negative signs are very negative, pointing to a society that is spiritually sick to its core. Let's move on to the positive spiritual signs and do some rejoicing!

One is the proclamation of the gospel to all the world (Matthew 24:14). This has occurred in the twentieth century as a result of modern technology such as short-wave radio and satellite television. With the advent of computer technology, the Word has been translated into hundreds, even thousands, of languages and dialects.

Another positive sign is the increasing understanding of Bible prophecy. Many of the prophecies concerning the end times were not even understood by the prophets who gave them. A good example is Daniel. He was mystified by many of the end-time prophecies which the Lord gave him. When he inquired about this, the Lord told him to stop worrying about it because the words are concealed and sealed up until the end time (Daniel 12:4,9).

As we get nearer to the day the Lord will return, we understand more and more of Bible prophecy. Some of the new understanding is due to the development of world events, such as the reestablishment of the nation of Israel. Other mysterious prophecies can now be understood due to modern technological developments. But some of our greater understanding is due to the illumination of the Holy Spirit—not the giving of new revelation, but the provision of enlightenment concerning the revelation that has already been given in God's Word.

One of the most glorious spiritual signs is the great outpouring of God's Spirit that the Church is receiving in these end times. The Bible prophesies that a great Holy Spirit empowerment will come in the latter days to enable Christians who are open to the Spirit's power to stand against the assaults of Satan.

In Joel 2:23 this is put in the imagery of an "early rain and a latter rain." The early rain was at Pentecost and continued through the early history of the Church when it was young and struggling to get established. The latter rain is occurring today as the true Church stands firm against the final assaults of Satan.

The Signs of Technology

The explosion of scientific knowledge and its technical application to communications, transportation, data processing, and weapons of war is definitely a sign of the soon return of the Lord (Daniel 12:4).

Consider, for example, how many prophecies we can now understand for the first time due to technological developments. Revelation 11 says that two great prophets of God will preach for three-and-a-half years during the first half of the Tribulation and then be killed by the Antichrist. Their bodies will lie in the streets of Jerusalem for three-and-a-half days and all the people in the world will look upon them (Revelation 11:3-13).

Prior to about 1955 it was very difficult to understand how all the people of the world could look upon two bodies lying in the streets of Jerusalem. Today we don't even stop to think about it because we know the capability of satellite television.

How could all the people of the world be given the mark of the beast (Revelation 13:16-18) before the invention of lasers and computers? How could the False Prophet make an image of the Antichrist that would appear to be alive (Revelation 13:14-15) before the development of robotics?

Jesus said that in the end times one of the signs will be "men fainting from fear and the expectation of the things which are coming upon the world; for the powers of the heavens will be shaken" (Luke 21:26). It sounds like the splitting of the atom to me—and the subsequent development of nuclear weapons.

The Signs of World Politics

Bible prophecy forecasts the coming together of a certain international pattern of nations in the end times.

The nation of Israel will once again exist, and all the nations of the world will seek to destroy the Jewish state (Zechariah 12:1-3). Particularly menacing to Israel will be a superpower located in "the remote parts of the north" (Ezekiel 38:6). This nation is identified in Ezekiel 38 in terms that can only be interpreted to mean modern-day Russia.

The resurgence of China as a superpower is also prophesied (Revelation 9:12-16; 16:12), as is the reunification of Europe (Daniel 7:7-8,24).

The world will be characterized by wars and rumors of wars (Matthew 24:6). The nations will also be afflicted with internal political strife that will often lead to "kingdom against kingdom," or civil war (Matthew 24:7). Lawlessness will increase everywhere (Matthew 24:12), a prophecy that has been fulfilled on the international scene with the advent of modern terrorism.

It is particularly interesting that the word translated "nation" in Matthew 24:7 ("nation will rise against nation") is the Greek word *ethnos*, which refers to an ethnic people group rather than a political nation-state. Since the breakup of the Soviet Union, we have never seen such outbreaks of ethnic violence—not only in the former Soviet republics, but also in areas like Yugoslavia, the Middle East, and even here in the United States, as manifested in the Los Angeles riots.

There is no doubt that we are living in a world where the end-time pattern has come together.

The Signs of Israel

The most important group of signs, more important than all the rest put together, is the group that pertains to the nation of Israel. These signs are outlined in detail in chapter 7.

The reason they are so important is because the Jewish people are God's prophetic time clock. By this I mean that very often when the Lord is revealing that an important event will take place in the future, He will point to the Jewish people and state that when a certain thing happens to them, the important event will also occur.

An example of this principle is found in Luke 21:24, where Jesus told His disciples to watch Jerusalem. His point was that Jerusalem would be conquered and then "trampled under foot by the Gentiles" until it was time for Him to return. In other words, He was saying that whenever the Jews win back the city of Jerusalem from the Gentiles, it will be a sure sign that His return is near.

The Romans conquered the city about 40 years after Jesus spoke these words. They were succeeded by the Byzantines, who were in turn succeeded by a host of Gentile nations until June 7, 1967, when the Jews finally reoccupied the city of Jerusalem for the first time in 1,897 years.

The Gentile world may not recognize the importance of this event, but the Orthodox Jews certainly do. They know the Old Testament prophecies and they therefore know that the Messiah is coming when they are back in their land and their city. That's why you can see banners all over Israel today that read, "Prepare for the Coming of the Messiah!"

Are You Ready?

God in His grace and mercy has provided us with a host of signs to prepare us for the soon return of His Son.

Prophecy is being fulfilled daily before our eyes. Jesus said in Luke 21:28 that when these signs *begin* to appear, "Straighten up and lift up your heads, because your redemption is drawing near."

We are living on borrowed time. Are you ready? Are you yearning? Can you say with Paul in 2 Timothy 4:7-8 that you are a candidate for a "crown of righteousness" because you have lived your life in the love of His appearing?

25

Second Coming Attitudes

Are You Yearning or Yawning?

Many scholars believe that one of the earliest prayers of the Church was "Maranatha!" (1 Corinthians 16:22).

That word is actually an Aramaic phrase that means "Our Lord come!" This prayer expresses a fact that is confirmed by many other Scriptures; namely, that the first-century Church had an ardent desire for the soon return of Jesus.

The Yawning of the Church

The twentieth-century Church seems to have lost that desire. The average Christian today does not pray "Maranatha!" He does not yearn for the return of the Lord.

Instead of yearning, he is yawning. Christendom at large is caught up in apathy regarding the return of

Jesus. And that is sad, for the Word says that the return of the Lord is our "blessed hope" (Titus 2:13).

Also, we are constantly admonished in the Scriptures to watch for the Lord's coming and to be ready. As Jesus Himself put it, "Be dressed in readiness, and keep your lamps alight" (Luke 12:35).

Reasons for Yearning

There are at least six reasons why every Christian should earnestly desire the soon return of Jesus:

1. *Glory for Jesus*—When Jesus returns He will get what He deserves—honor, glory, and power. He was humiliated in history, and He will be vindicated and glorified in history. He will be the King of kings and Lord of lords, and He will reign over all the world from Mount Zion in Jerusalem (Isaiah 24:21-23).

2. *Defeat for Satan*—When Jesus returns, Satan will receive what he deserves—defeat, dishonor, and humiliation. The fate of Satan was sealed by the Cross, but his nefarious activities will not cease until the Lord returns. At that time, he will be crushed (Romans 16:20 and Revelation 20:1-3).

3. *Refreshment for the Earth*—When Jesus returns, the creation will receive what it has been promised—restoration. The earth itself will be renovated by earthquakes and supernatural phenomena in the heavens. The result will be a beautified earth. The destructive forces of nature will be curtailed. Deserts will bloom. The plant and animal kingdoms will be redeemed. Poisonous plants and animals will cease to be poisonous. Carnivorous animals will become herbivorous. All of nature will cease to strive against itself. Instead, it will work together harmoniously to the benefit of Man and the glory of God. (See Isaiah 11:6-9; 35:1-10; 65:17-25; Acts 3:19-21; Romans 8:18-23.)

4. *Peace for the Nations*—When Jesus returns, the nations will receive what they have been promised—

peace, righteousness, and justice. (See Isaiah 9:6-7; 11:3-5; Micah 4:1-7.)

5. *Primacy for the Jews*—When Jesus returns, the Jews will receive what they have been promised— salvation and primacy. Near the end of the Tribulation, a remnant of the Jews will accept Jesus as their Messiah. This remnant will be gathered and established in Israel as the prime nation of the world. (See Hosea 2:14-20; Isaiah 60-62; Romans 9-11).

6. *Blessings for the Church*—When Jesus returns, the saints will receive what they have been promised— glorified bodies, a redeemed earth, ruling power over the nations, and reunification with loved ones who are already with the Lord. (See Matthew 5:5; Philippians 3:20-21; 1 Thessalonians 4:14; Revelation 2:26-27).

These six reasons make it clear that every Christian should be earnestly desiring the return of the Lord. Yet apathy prevails. Why?

Reasons for Apathy

I have found four reasons for the apathy and indifference that characterize the Christian community concerning the return of Jesus: 1) unbelief; 2) ignorance; 3) fear; and 4) carnality.

Many professing Christians simply do not believe that Jesus will ever return. Most of these are people with a liberal view of Scripture. They have spiritualized away the meaning of the Second Coming, just as they have spiritualized the virgin birth and the miracles.

Probably most Christians are just ignorant about what will happen when the Lord returns. As a result, they cannot get excited about an event they know nothing about. I was in this category for 30 years. Although I attended church faithfully, my church ignored the teaching and preaching of the Prophetic Word.

Some Christians fear the return of Jesus, and so they try to repress the thought that He might break from the heavens at any moment. They fear He might return on one of their "bad" days or when they have an "unconfessed sin" on their conscience. These people are caught up in works salvation. They do not understand that they are saved by grace and that "there is therefore now no condemnation for those who are in Christ Jesus" (Romans 8:1).

Finally, there are many carnal Christians who cannot get excited about the coming of the Lord because they are in love with the world. They are walking with one foot in the Church and one foot in the country club. They want the Lord to come, but they want Him to come when they are 80 years old and have experienced all that this world has to offer. In other words, they want Him to come, but they don't want Him to mess up their lives.

Indications of the Message

The message that Jesus is coming soon is like a two-edged sword. It speaks to both believers and unbelievers.

The message to unbelievers is "flee from the wrath [that is] to come" (Matthew 3:7) by fleeing into the loving arms of Jesus *now* (Matthew 11:28-30). The message to believers is to stop playing church and get serious about their Christian commitment by dedicating their lives to holiness (1 Peter 1:13-16).

The Challenge to Unbelievers

If you are an unbeliever still struggling with God, I urge you to carefully contemplate the evidence of fulfilled prophecy that has been presented in this book. Consider how it validates the Bible as the Word of God and confirms Jesus as the Son of God.

God loves you (John 3:16). He wants you to become an heir of the promises contained in His master plan

(2 Peter 3:9). I appeal to you to reach out in faith to Him (Hebrews 11:6). Humble yourself before Him (2 Peter 5:6-7). Confess your sins (Romans 10:9). Ask Him to forgive you and save you (Acts 2:21). Receive His Son, Jesus, as your Lord and Savior (John 14:6). And then seek out a fellowship of believers where you can begin to grow in the Lord (Hebrews 10:25).

Receiving Jesus into your life is not just a way of preparing for His soon return. It will have an impact upon your life here and now. He will give you the gift of His Holy Spirit (Romans 5:5), and the Spirit will begin to empower and strengthen you for victorious living as an "overcomer" (1 John 5:1-5).

The Challenge to Believers

If you are a believer, you can no longer plead ignorance regarding the marvelous promises of God that will be fulfilled when Jesus returns. You now know the master plan.

I hope this book has also dispelled any fear that you might have had about the certainty of your salvation. I have repeatedly emphasized the amazing grace of God. You need to trust in the Lord's faithfulness.

So let me ask you: Are you still apathetic? If so, why? If it's not due to fear or ignorance, is it due to unbelief or carnality?

I challenge you to allow the spotlight of the Holy Spirit to shine upon your heart and reveal to you the reason for any apathy you may still have regarding the soon return of Jesus.

If your problem is unbelief regarding Bible prophecy, then I challenge you to accept in faith the validity of *all* God's Word—and not just the truth of the gospel message (2 Timothy 3:16-17). Consider the fact than when you call into question any of God's Word, you challenge the validity of all of it. We are not free to pick and choose what we want to believe in God's Word. We are called to accept all of it in faith (Habakkuk 2:4; Romans 1:17).

If your problem is carnality because you have compromised with the world, then I challenge you to commit your life to holiness by making Jesus the Lord of every aspect of your being (Romans 13:12-14). Take an inventory of your life and ask: "Is Jesus the Lord of my movies? Is He the Lord of my TV? What about my music and my reading material? Is He the Lord of my job? My marriage? My recreation? Is He the Lord of *anything* in my life?"

I can think of one other concern about the return of Jesus that may be prompting an apathetic attitude on your part. Perhaps you are saying to yourself, "I want the Lord to come, but I want to see certain family members or friends give their lives to Jesus first."

If that is your attitude, please don't feel bad about it. It is a spiritually legitimate attitude. You *should* be concerned about the eternal destiny of your family members and friends.

Just keep in mind that the Lord's timing for His return will be perfect, so turn your concern for family and friends over to the Lord and let Him deal with it. He wants your heart to be filled with unqualified anticipation for His soon return (2 Timothy 4:7-8).

Something Personal

I have presented many reasons why every Christian should earnestly desire the soon return of Jesus.

In addition to those reasons, I want to add a personal one. I want Jesus to come back because . . .

> I want to be with Him.
> I want to bask in the presence of His love
>   and holiness.
> I want to see the glory of God in His face.

I want to kiss the nail-scarred hands and
   say, "Thank You"
      for dying for me,
      for forgiving me,
      for changing me,
      for guiding me,
      for comforting me,
      for giving my life
         meaning and purpose.

And I want to join the saints and the heavenly host
in singing, "Worthy is the Lamb."

MARANATHA!

Appendices
Index

Appendix 1

A Summary of
First Coming Prophecies

There are over 300 prophecies in the Old Testament about the First Coming of the Messiah, but many of these are repetitious. When the repetitious ones are deleted, we are left with 108 specifically different prophecies, all of which were fulilled in the life of Jesus of Nazareth.

The fulfillment of so many prophecies in the life of one person is overwhelming proof that Jesus is the Messiah of God. The odds of so many prophecies being fulfilled coincidentally in the life of any person is beyond the realm of probability. Fulfilled prophecy is thus one of the most substantial proofs that Jesus was who He said He was—namely, the anointed Son of God (Mark 14:62-63).

In the following outline, only one source is given for each prophecy, but keep in mind that some of the prophecies are repeated several times in the Old Testament Scriptures.

A detailed listing of both Old Testament and New Testament verses pertaining to these prophecies can be found in a book published by Lamb & Lion Ministries called, *The Christ in Prophecy Study Guide.*

Old Testament Source	THE PROPHECY	New Testament Fulfillment
A. The Messiah's Lineage		
Gen. 9:26	1) From the Shemite branch of humanity	Luke 3:36
Gen. 12:3	2) Through Abraham	Matt. 1:1
Gen. 17:21	3) Through Abraham's son, Isaac	Luke 3:34
Gen. 28:14	4) Through Isaac's son, Jacob	Luke 3:34
Gen. 49:8	5) Through the tribe of Judah	Luke 3:33ff.
Isa. 11:1	6) Through the family of Jesse	Luke 3:32
Jer. 23:5	7) Through the house of David	Luke 3:31ff.
B. The Messiah's Birth and Childhood		
Gen. 49:10	1) Timing of birth. According to the Talmud, in about A.D. 7 the Romans removed the power of the Sanhedrin Council in Judah to pronounce the death penalty—thus the scepter (power) passed from Judah. Jesus had been born in 4 B.C., during the reign of Herod (Matt. 2:1), so "Shiloh" (a messianic title) had come shortly before the scepter departed—just as prophesied.	
Mic. 5:2	2) Place of birth	Matt. 2:1
Isa. 9:6	3) Born in the flesh	Luke 2:11
Isa. 7:14	4) Born of a virgin	Luke 1:34ff.
Isa. 7:14	5) Divine name	Matt. 1:21
Psa. 72:10ff.	6) Presented with gifts at birth	Matt. 2:1-12
Jer. 31:15	7) Infants massacred	Matt. 2:16
Hos. 11:1	8) Sojourn in Egypt	Matt. 2:14ff.
Isa. 11:1*	9) Residence in Nazareth	Matt. 2:23
Isa. 53:2	10) Grow up in obscurity and poverty.	Mark 6:3
Isa. 11:1ff.	11) Spirit-filled and anointed from birth	Luke 2:46ff.

---

*Matthew's reference is uncertain. Some believe it is derived from Isaiah 53:4, where the Messiah is referred to as a pain bearer. The word for pain here is "natzri." Others say Matthew is referring to Isaiah 11:1, where the Messiah is referred to as a "neser"—that is, a "branch" of Jesse.

Old Testament Source	THE PROPHECY	New Testament Fulfillment

C. The Messiah's Life and Ministry

Isa. 40:3	1) Preceded by a prophet who would prepare His way	Matt. 3:1ff.
Isa. 42:1	2) Receive a special anointing by the Holy Spirit	Luke 3:22
Gen. 3:15	3) Do battle with Satan	Matt. 4:1ff.
Psa. 91:11	4) Receive the ministry of angels	Matt. 4:11
Isa. 9:1	5) Ministry centered in Galilee	Matt. 4:13
Isa. 42:2	6) Unpretentious ministry	John 6:15
Isa. 53:2	7) Power of ministry not based on personal appearance	Matt. 7:28ff.
Psa. 40:9	8) Preacher	Matt. 4:17
Psa. 78:2	9) Teacher in parables	Matt. 13:34ff.
Deu. 18:15ff.	10) Prophet	Matt. 21:11
Isa. 33:22	11) Judge	John 5:30
Isa. 11:2	12) Miracle-worker	John 3:2
Psa. 109:4	13) Man of prayer	Luke 18:1
Psa. 22:9ff.	14) A Man whose reliance and trust is in God	John 5:19
Psa. 40:8	15) A Man of obedience	John 4:34
Isa. 11:2	16) A Man of knowledge, wisdom, and understanding	Matt. 13:54
Isa. 11:2	17) A Man of counsel	John 3:1-4
Zec. 9:9	18) Humble in spirit	Phil. 2:8
Psa. 145:8	19) Patient	1 Tim. 1:16
Psa. 103:17	20) Loving and merciful	John 15:13
Psa. 69:9	21) Zeal for God's house in Jerusalem	John 2:14ff.
Isa. 61:1-2	22) Proclaim a Jubilee	Luke 4:17ff.
Isa. 61:1	23) Preach the gospel to the poor	Matt. 11:4-5
Isa. 61:1	24) Comfort the brokenhearted	Matt. 11:28
Isa. 61:1	25) Proclaim liberty to captives	Matt. 8:16
Isa. 42:3	26) Minister to broken lives	Luke 5:30ff.
Isa. 53:5	27) Heal the sick	Matt. 8:16ff.
Isa. 35:5-6	28) Heal those with special afflictions	Matt. 11:4ff.
Psa. 69:4	29) Hated without cause	John 15:24ff.
Psa. 69:7-8	30) Despised and rejected by His own people, the Jews	John 1:11
Isa. 29:13	31) Rejected by the Jews due to exaltation of tradition	Mark 7:6ff.

Old Testament Source	THE PROPHECY	New Testament Fulfillment
Psa. 8:2	32) Praised by babes and infants	Matt. 21:15ff.
Isa. 49:6	33) Offered to the Gentiles	John 1:12
Hos. 2:23	34) Accepted by the Gentiles	Acts 28:28

D. The Messiah's Nature

Mic. 5:2	1) Eternal	John 1:1
Isa. 9:6	2) Divine	John 10:30
Psa. 8:5	3) Human	John 1:14
Psa. 2:7	4) Son of God	Matt. 3:17
Dan. 7:13	5) Son of Man	Matt. 8:20
Psa. 2:2	6) Christ, the Anointed One	Luke 2:10ff.
Psa. 110:1	7) Lord	John 13:13
Isa. 11:2-3	8) God-centered	John 17:4
Isa. 5:16	9) Holy	John 6:69
Isa. 53:11	10) Righteous	Acts 7:52
Psa. 89:1-2	11) Faithful and true witness	Rev. 3:14
Isa. 42:1	12) Servant of God	Phil. 2:6-7
Psa. 23:1	13) A loving shepherd	John 10:11
Isa. 53:7	14) A sacrificial lamb	John 1:29
Isa. 53:4-6	15) A sin-bearer	1 Pet. 2:24
Isa. 53:10	16) A guilt offering	Heb. 9:13ff.
Isa. 42:6	17) Embodiment of God's Redemptive Covenant	John 22:20

E. The Messiah's Death

Dan. 9:25ff.	1) Timing of death. The prophecy states that the Messiah will die 69 weeks of years (483 years) after the edict is issued to rebuild Jersualem. The edict was issued by Artaxerxes in 445 B.C., and 483 lunar years later, Jesus was crucified in Jerusalem.	
Zec. 9:9	2) Triumphal entry into Jerusalem	John 12:12ff.
Isa. 53:3ff.	3) Experience profound grief and agony	Matt. 26:37ff.
Psa. 41:9	4) Betrayal by a friend who would eat with Him	Matt. 26:30ff.
Zec. 11:12	5) Betrayal for 30 pieces of silver	Matt. 26:14ff.
Zec. 11:13	6) Disposition of the betrayal money	Matt. 27:3ff.
Zec. 13:7	7) Forsaken by His disciples	Matt. 26:55ff.
Psa. 35:11ff.	8) Accused by false witnesses	Matt. 26:59
Isa. 53:7	9) Silent before His accusers	Matt. 27:14
Isa. 50:6	10) Spat upon	Matt. 26:67

Old Testament Source	THE PROPHECY	New Testament Fulfillment
Mic. 5:1	11) Stricken	Matt. 26:67
Isa. 50:6	12) Scourged	Matt. 27:26
Isa. 52:14	13) Face beaten to a pulp	Matt. 27:30
Isa. 50:6	14) Beard plucked. There is no specific recorded fulfillment of this prophecy, but it was likely one of the tortures inflicted upon Jesus by the Roman soldiers	
Isa. 50:6	15) Humiliated	Mark 15:17ff.
Psa. 22:15	16) Physical exhaustion	Luke 23:26
Psa. 22:16	17) Crucified	Luke 23:33
Isa. 53:12	18) Identified with sinners	Mark 15:27
Psa. 22:6-8	19) Object of scorn and ridicule	Luke 23:35ff.
Psa. 22:15	20) Experienced thirst	John 19:28
Psa. 69:21	21) Given vinegar to drink	Matt. 27:48
Psa. 38:11	22) Friends stand far away	Luke 23:49
Psa. 22:17	23) Stared at	Luke 23:35
Psa. 22:18	24) Clothing divided by persecutors	John 19:23
Psa. 22:18	25) Lots cast for robe	John 19:23ff.
Amos 8:9	26) Darkness at noon	Matt. 27:45
Psa. 22:1	27) Cry of disorientation due to separation from God	Matt. 27:46
Psa. 109:4	28) Pray for persecutors	Luke 23:34
Psa. 22:31*	29) Cry of victory	John 19:30
Psa. 31:5	30) Voluntary release of spirit	Luke 23:46
Psa. 34:20	31) No bones broken	John 19:32ff.
Zec. 12:10	32) Pierced in the side	John 19:34
Psa. 22:14	33) Death by a broken heart	John 19:34**
Isa. 53:9	34) Buried in a rich man's grave	Matt. 27:57ff.

F. The Messiah's Resurrection and Ascension

Psa. 16:10	1) Resurrection	Mark 16:6
Psa. 68:18	2) Ascension	Acts 1:9
Psa. 110:1	3) Exaltation at the right hand of God	Mark 16:19
Psa. 110:4	4) Serve as a High Priest	Heb. 6:20
Psa. 2:1-2	5) Continue to be despised by the nations	1 Jn. 5:19

---

*The phrase, "He has performed it" literally means, "He has finished it."

**The separation of the blood and water is a sign of a ruptured heart.

Appendix 2

Recommended Books on Bible Prophecy

The best overall book on Bible prophecy that has ever been published is *Things to Come* by Dwight Pentecost. It is scholarly and comprehensive, written for serious, college-level readers.

Surveys

For the more general reader, the best survey of end-time Bible prophecy is Leon Wood's book *The Bible and Future Events*. Other very readable surveys are *The Final Chapter* by S. Maxwell Coder and *A Survey of Bible Prophecy* by R. Ludwigson. *The King Is Coming* by H.L. Willmington presents an overview of end-time events in a very unique and easy-to-follow outline form.

A book published by Lamb & Lion Ministries, *The Christ in Prophecy Study Guide,* presents an analytical survey of all messianic prophecy contained in both the

Old and New Testaments. Another indispensable reference volume is *All the Messianic Prophecies of the Bible* by Herbert Lockyer.

A survey book intended for the serious student is Arnold Fruchtenbaum's encyclopedic study of Tribulation events, which bears the strange title *The Footsteps of the Messiah*. It focuses on showing the sequence of end-time events and their relationship to each other.

A brief and fascinating survey book full of penetrating insights is *What on Earth Is God Doing?* It was written by Renald Showers, a gifted teacher and writer who serves the Friends of Israel Gospel Ministry. The book presents a capsule overview of God's purposes in history from start to finish.

Interpretation

Nothing is more important to the understanding of Bible prophecy than the principles of interpretation that are applied to it. An excellent introductory book for the general reader is *How to Study Bible Prophecy for Yourself* by Tim LaHaye.

The most profound book ever written on the topic is *The Interpretation of Prophecy* by Paul Lee Tan. This book is an essential tool for any serious student of prophecy.

Viewpoints

The best introduction to the various and often confusing viewpoints of end-time prophecy is a book by Robert Lightner called *The Last Days Handbook*.

A very thought-provoking book on the topic is one edited by Robert G. Clouse, titled *The Meaning of the Millennium*. It contains four viewpoints presented by advocates of those viewpoints. A scholarly presentation of the various views is contained in John Walvoord's book *The Millennial Kingdom*.

For a classic presentation of the fundamentals of premillennial theology, the book to read is *The Basis of the Premillennial Faith* by Charles Ryrie. It is brief and incisive, and it is written with an irenic spirit.

Revelation

Many excellent studies have been published about the book of Revelation. For the general reader, the two best ones are *Revelation Illustrated and Made Plain* by Tim LaHaye and *There's a New World Coming* by Hal Lindsey. Lindsey's book is the best one he has ever written.

For those who desire to dig deeper, I recommend *The Revelation Record* by Henry Morris, the distinguished founder of the Institute for Creation Research. An outstanding introduction to the book of Revelation and the various methods of interpreting it is supplied by Merrill Tenney in his remarkably balanced volume *Interpreting Revelation*.

Daniel

It is more difficult to find good commentaries on the book of Daniel. The best is by Renald Showers. It is titled *The Most High God*. A lighter book that is both fun to read and inspirational in character is *Daniel: God's Man in a Secular Society* by Donald Campbell. It is designed to serve as a study guide for Bible study groups.

No book of the Bible has been attacked as viciously by theological liberals as the book of Daniel. A tremendous defense of the book's integrity can be found in a volume called *Daniel in the Critic's Den* by Josh McDowell.

Old Testament Prophets

A magnificent introduction to all the Old Testament prophets is provided by Leon Wood in his exceptional book *The Prophets of Israel*.

One of the finest commentators on the Old Testament prophets is Charles Feinberg, a Messianic Jew. His works include *God Remembers: A Study of Zechariah*, *Jeremiah: A Commentary*, and *The Prophecy of Ezekiel*. A good introduction to Isaiah can be found in the book by Herbert Wolf titled *Interpreting Isaiah*.

There are a number of good books about the Minor Prophets. Two that are designed for the general reader are *Major Truths from the Minor Prophets* by John Hunter and *Will We Ever Catch Up with the Bible?* by David Hubbard.

Israel

The best panoramic survey of Israel in prophecy is contained in Richard Booker's outstanding study *Blow the Trumpet in Zion*.

A good book that relates prophecy to the history of Israel, particularly modern history, is called *It Is No Dream*. It was written by Elwood McQuaid, the director of the Friends of Israel Gospel Ministry. Charles Feinberg has also produced an excellent volume that mixes prophecy with history. It is titled *Israel: At the Center of History and Revelation*.

The Rapture

The important controversy over the timing of the Rapture has been best addressed by John Walvoord in two of his books: *The Rapture Question* and *The Blessed Hope and the Tribulation*. Walvoord is the former president of Dallas Theological Seminary. Another fine book on the topic is *The Rapture* by Hal Lindsey. The most recent volume is one by Tim LaHaye titled *No Fear of the Storm*.

Symbolic Prophecy

Perhaps the least-understood area of prophecy is symbolic prophecy, sometimes called prophecy in type.

About half of Herbert Lockyer's book *All the Messianic Prophecies of the Bible* is dedicated to this important topic.

Two books concerning symbolic prophecy that are easy to read and are full of useful insights are *Christ in the Tabernacle* by Louis Talbot and *Jesus in the Feasts of Israel* by Richard Booker.

Signs of the Times

This is a field that attracts many sensationalist writers. There is an abundance of books, but few good ones. The most comprehensive is *World War III: Signs of the Impending Battle of Armageddon* by John Wesley White.

A volume that is also comprehensive but exceptionally brief is *Signs of the Second Coming* by Robert G. Witty. The newest study, and an excellent one, is by Henry Morris. It is titled *Creation and the Second Coming*.

Children

Only one book has ever been written for children concerning end-time prophecy. It was published by Harvest House in 1992. The title is *Jesus Is Coming Again!* It is beautifully illustrated in full color.

Bibles

The first study Bible ever published came out in 1909. It is still one of the best-selling study Bibles in the world. It was produced by a Dallas pastor named C.I. Scofield and is called *The Scofield Study Bible*. It has been revised and updated regularly over the years by an editorial committee representing a premillennial, pre-Tribulational viewpoint.

A newer study Bible that presents the same view of the passages related to end-time prophecy is *The Ryrie*

Study Bible. Both the Scofield and Ryrie commentaries are available with a variety of translations.

The Living Bible Paraphrased, though not a typical study Bible, is nonetheless an interpretive Bible that reflects a premillennial interpretation of all key prophetic passages.

Classics

The greatest and most enduring classic on the return of Jesus is William E. Blackstone's book *Jesus Is Coming.* It was written in 1878. The third revised edition of 1908 has been recently republished by Kregel, with an introduction by John Walvoord. The modern-day classic is Hal Lindsey's *The Late Great Planet Earth.* The New York Times has certified that it was the number one best-selling book in the world (with the exception of the Bible) for ten years, between 1970 and 1980!

Perhaps the most unusual book ever published on Bible prophecy is *Dispensational Truth* by Clarence Larkin. Larkin was a draftsman who devoted his talents to illustrating prophetic concepts with fascinating charts and diagrams. This is a classic that will keep you up all night!

Index

About the Author

Dr. David R. Reagan is the Evangelist for Lamb & Lion Ministries, a prophetic ministry located in the Dallas, Texas, area.

Before founding the ministry in 1980, Dr. Reagan served for 20 years as a university professor, teaching international law and politics. Throughout that time he was an ardent student of the Bible.

Since 1980 Dr. Reagan has taught Bible prophecy in meetings and seminars held all across America and around the world.

His daily radio program, "Christ in Prophecy," is broadcast throughout the United States.

He has made many trips to Israel and is considered an expert on Middle East politics and Israel in Bible prophecy.

Dr. Reagan has been gifted with the skill to communicate complex ideas in simple, understandable terms. He is the author of several books, including the only children's book ever published about end-time Bible prophecy, titled *Jesus Is Coming Again!* (Harvest House, 1992).

Dr. Reagan and his wife, Ann, live in a Dallas suburb. They are the parents of two daughters and have four grandchildren.

For a catalog of Dr. Reagan's tapes and publications, write to Lamb & Lion Ministries, P.O. Box 919, McKinney, Texas 75069, U.S.A.

Other Good Harvest House Reading

ONE WORLD UNDER ANTICHRIST
by *Peter Lalonde*

Author Peter Lalonde takes you into the stories behind the news, putting events in context of biblical prophecy and examining how these events are connected to each other and to the much-talked-about New World Order. Highly readable and well-documented, *One World Under Antichrist* cuts through the confusion while offering hope and challenge for the Christian who wants a deeper understanding of last days' events.

JESUS IS COMING AGAIN!
by *David Reagan*

Now your children, ages 3-10, can know the faith-enriching experience of Bible prophecy through simple words and colorful, easy-to-understand illustrations. *Jesus Is Coming Again!* helps kids look forward to Jesus' return without getting lost in difficult concepts and complicated language.

READY TO REBUILD
by *Thomas Ice and Randall Price*

After centuries of persecution and dispersion, Jews are back in their land and pursuing the rebuilding of the Temple with increasing fervor. This fascinating, fast-moving overview of contemporary events shows why the Temple is significant in Bible prophecy and how, more than ever, Israel is *Ready to Rebuild*.

HOW TO STUDY THE BIBLE FOR YOURSELF
by *Tim LaHaye*

This excellent book provides fascinating study helps and charts that will make personal Bible study more interesting and exciting. A three-year program is outlined for a good working knowledge of the Bible.

Dear Reader:

We would appreciate hearing from you regarding this Harvest House nonfiction book. It will enable us to continue to give you the best in Christian publishing.

1. What most influenced you to purchase *The Master Plan*?
   ☐ Author   ☐ Recommendations
   ☐ Subject matter   ☐ Cover/Title
   ☐ Backcover copy   ☐ _____

2. Where did you purchase this book?
   ☐ Christian bookstore   ☐ Grocery store
   ☐ General bookstore   ☐ Other
   ☐ Department store

3. Your overall rating of this book:
   ☐ Excellent ☐ Very good ☐ Good ☐ Fair ☐ Poor

4. How likely would you be to purchase other books by this author?
   ☐ Very likely   ☐ Not very likely
   ☐ Somewhat likely   ☐ Not at all

5. What types of books most interest you?
   (check all that apply)
   ☐ Women's Books   ☐ Fiction
   ☐ Marriage Books   ☐ Biographies
   ☐ Current Issues   ☐ Children's Books
   ☐ Self Help/Psychology   ☐ Youth Books
   ☐ Bible Studies   ☐ Other _____

6. Please check the box next to your age group.
   ☐ Under 18   ☐ 25-34   ☐ 45-54
   ☐ 18-24   ☐ 35-44   ☐ 55 and over

Mail to: Editorial Director
Harvest House Publishers
1075 Arrowsmith
Eugene, OR 97402

Name _____

Address _____

City _____ State _____ Zip _____

**Thank you for helping us to help you
in future publications!**